Living by the Light of the Moon

2018 Moon Book

Beatrex Quntanna

Disclaimer

Before following any Yoga advice or practice suggested by this book, it is recommended that you consult your doctor as to its suitability, especially if you suffer from any health problems or special conditions. The publishers, the author, and associates cannot accept responsibility for any injuries or damage incurred as a result of following the exercises in this book, or using any of the therapeutic methods described or mentioned.

ISBN 978-0-9625292-8-3

Printed in the United States of America

ART ALA CARTE PUBLISHING
760-944-6020
beatrex@cox.net
www.beatrex.com

This book is dedicated to
the memory of Master Teacher
and Mystic Nancy Tappe—my dear
friend and mentor—who inspired me
and encouraged me to manifest
the teachings in this book.
Thank you, Nancy.

Acknowledgments

I wish to thank Jennifer Masters for the cover art and for her ability to capture the *Illumination* theme with her magical graphic art. Michelenne Crab for her personal support, research gathering, and for her tech support for the last 17 years. Michael Makay for the daily Tibetan Numerology intentions that inspire and direct us to make the most of each day. Katherine Sale for the astrological calculations for the entire year. Jennifer "Tashi" Vause, R.Y.T., for *Sky Power Yoga*, taking the time to determine yoga poses for each moon. So much fun to add the physical domain to astrology! Kaliani Devinne for contributing the goddess profiles that correspond to each moon cycle and the moon charts. Jill Estensen for sharing aspects from *Dimensional Astrology* that add an innovative approach to the Sabian Symbols, experiencing the degrees and the polarity that they create for each moon phase. Candice Covington for her approach to the elements. Ann Meyer for the freedom affirmations from *Teaching of the Inner Christ*. Tashi and Melinda Pajak for their sense of refinement and attention to detail. *Special thanks to the countless students who come to Moon Class—without you this teaching would not exist!*

Production Credits

Art Direction, Book Design, Cover Art, and Video Editing (*How to Use the Moon Book* video class series)
 Jennifer Masters
 JenniferMastersCreative.com

Daily Tibetan Numerology
 Michael Makay
 mbmakay@gmail.com

Sabian Symbols *Dimensional Astrology*
 Jill Estensen
 intuvision@roadrunner.com

Astrological Calculations
 Katherine Sale, M.S.W., M.Ac.
 StargazerKat@gmail.com

Goddess Profiles
 Kaliani Devinne
 StepsOnTheSacredSpiral.blogspot.com

Sky Power Yoga
 Jennifer "Tashi" Vause, R.Y.T.
 yogatashi@yahoo.com

Video Production (*How to Use the Moon Book* video class series)
 Melinda Pajak
 www.MelindaPajak.com
 www.BlueMoonAcademy.com

Table of Contents

About the Art

Meditating on the Tibetan numerology of eleven left me with a big creative blank, until Beatrex talked about how the number eleven encompasses vastness, the totality of everything, portals, and the birth of new universes upon universes ... and it hit me, like a "Big Bang!" I got it. The circle, spiral, and infinite repetition became my visual themes. I spent time researching fractal designs, kaleidoscopes, and mandala art. The stars of our Universe are scattered throughout these pages, along with the building blocks of *everything*, like spirals of DNA and the Elements (earth, air, fire, water, and aether/spirit).

I created the main kaleidoscope/mandala/portal/universe images digitally in Photoshop, incorporating bits and pieces of the imagery from all the editions of *Living by the Light of the Moon* I've had the pleasure of working on to this point. They are thematically based on the zodiac symbols and corresponding concepts. They each had their own evolutionary process—it took time to pull together all of the pieces, with the final picture only emerging into being at the very end. I hope you enjoy exploring them as much as I enjoyed creating them.

—Jennifer Masters
Artist, Illustrator, Creative

The Importance of Cycles

The Moon is the keeper of the secrets of life and its cycles set the stage for successful living. Beatrex has developed a valuable collection of knowledge about how to use the cycles of the Moon to enhance the quality of your life. This workbook reveals those secrets and supports you in implementing them. Each cycle offers a different combination of light energy to give you the chance to grow harmoniously into wholeness. Following the luminaries, the Sun and the Moon, through the zodiac and noting the cycles of illumination and reflection can bring you to a deeper creative experience of life. The Moon is the great cosmic architect—the builder and the dissolver of form. Full Moons are about dissolving and New Moons are about building. This workbook will assist you in knowing what and when to build and what and when to dissolve with activities for each cycle of the Moon throughout 2018.

Life, at the highest spiritual level, moves beyond time and uses cycles to increase your ability to actualize your full potential. Cycles are in charge of your personal development; while time is in charge of the change in direction that happens when you evolve by trusting in divine timing. This workbook synthesizes techniques that allow for the power of development and direction to occur in the entire spectrum of wholeness. Each zodiac sign holds the knowledge necessary to integrate an aspect of yourself to become whole. As the Moon and the Sun travel around our planet each month, a different aspect of self-development is presented to you via the zodiac sign constellation that it visits.

The Year of Illumination keeps your manifesting ability available to you in each moment. The more you manifest—by allowing the bliss from your spiritual essence to come forward—the less you suffer. Give up being devoted to the past and embark on new frontiers. Adjust and recalibrate the core of your being. This workbook instructs you on how to manifest and to recalibrate so that the power of illumination becomes your reality in 2018.

When the Moon is Full

It is time to set yourself free when the Moon is full and in direct opposition to the Sun. This polarity dissolves anything that stands in the way of your personal recalibration. Sixty hours before a full moon you may experience tension as the Sun and the Moon oppose each other. Learn to understand the opposite natures without feeling the need to separate them. Find the middle ground so that you are not manipulated by polarity as the integration of opposites creates the unity that creates harmony.

The polarity themes are on each full moon's page. Use the astrological theme to inspire you to renew your life by writing a freedom list. Light a candle and read your list out loud. Place your freedom list under a circle-shaped mirror and put your candle on top of the mirror. Make sure to use a candle in glass—a votive or seven-day candle—to protect from fire. Place outside in the moonlight or in a special place in your home. Let the candle burn out. When your candle is finished burning, your list is in operation. Empty space allows manifestation to occur. Before writing your list you might want to look over the full moon cycle's trigger points to see if there is anything you need to let go of first. Remember recalibration allows you to live without resistance.

When the Moon is New

When the Moon is new, it is in the same sign as the Sun. This unites the power of the magnetic and the dynamic fields that are in perfect resonance for manifesting. This is a potent time to make your desires known by writing your manifesting list. Use the astrological theme to write your list like a child who is writing to Santa Claus. Be comfortable with extending your list's boundaries beyond what you believe is possible by thinking: *This, or something better than this, comes to me in an easy and pleasurable way for the good of all concerned.* Then light a candle and read your list out loud. Place it under an eight-sided mirror and put your candle on top of the mirror. Make sure to use a candle in glass—a votive or seven-day candle—to protect from fire. Place outside in the moonlight or in a special place in your home. Let the candle burn out. By the time the candle burns out, your list is in operation.

How To Use This Book

Your Time Zone

All times listed in the book are local to the Pacific time zone. Add or subtract hours accordingly to adjust times for your time zone. It is best to do your manifestation and freedom ceremonies at the specific times noted.

These Sections Will Help You to Live by the Light of the Moon

Planetary Highlights

This section explains the planets and how they will affect your life each month. It does not contain all of the aspects; it simply highlights points of interest that promote personal growth during each month. If you are interested in more study, take an astrology class. If you are an astrologer and want more information, we have provided a chart for each moon phase for your convenience.

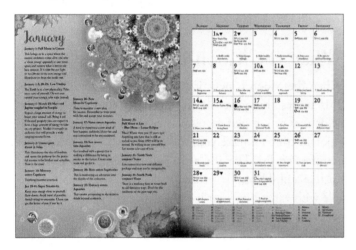

The Monthly Calendar

This section provides you with a monthly overview and keeps you connected to the lunar, solar, and planetary cycles. It lets you know when the Moon is void-of-course, when it moves into a new sign, when the Sun and planets change signs, and when a planet goes retrograde or stationary direct (shown by the $\frac{S}{D}$ symbol). The calendar also has the Tibetan Numerology of the Day, along with an affirmation, to help you align with the energy and set your intentions for the day.

Void Moon

When the Moon is void-of-course, it has made its last major aspect in a sign and stays void until it enters the next sign. When the Moon is void-of-course, you will see the icon

V/C on the calendar. This is not a good time to start new projects, relationships, or to take trips, unless you intend to never follow through. When the Moon ☽ enters a new sign, you will see this arrow ➡ It will be followed by the symbol for the new sign and the time that the Moon enters it.

Super-Sensitivity ▲

This happens when the Moon travels across the sky, hits the center of the galaxy, and connects with a fixed star. When this happens the atmosphere becomes chaotic. An extra amount of energy pours down in a spiral at a very fast speed making it difficult to focus. This fragility can make you depressed, anxious, dizzy, and accident-prone. It is a good idea to keep your thought process away from this energy. This is global, not personal.

Low-Vitality ▼

This happens when the Moon is directly opposite the center of the galaxy. When this fixed-star opposition occurs, the Earth becomes very fragile and gets depleted. This leads to exhaustion in our physical bodies and is a sign for us to nurture ourselves by resting. The depletion can create Earth changes. Endings can also happen and resistance to these completions will bring on exhaustion. Best to detach and let go.

The Sun

Each month you will see the icon for the Sun ☉ with an arrow ➡ indicating when the Sun enters a new sign. When the Sun changes signs, the climate of energy takes on a new theme for your personal development. Look for the Sun icon, with an arrow followed by an astrological sign, to indicate sign change and time.

Planets

Planets also change signs and move in retrograde and direct motions. Retrograde planets are next to the date in each day's box followed by retrograde icon ℞. In the middle of each box is information about planetary changes of time and direction.

Goddesses

When the Moon enters a new zodiac sign, a changing of guardians occurs. Deep within each sign lives a goddess who is the keeper of this cyclical domain. This archetype's assignment is to hold the space for an aspect of wholeness to actualize.

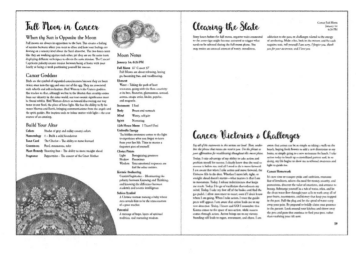

Build Your Altar

An altar is an outer focus for inner work. Esoteric coordinates such as Tarot cards, flowers, colors, gemstones, fragrances, and numerology are provided as an enhancement to better assist you in working with each moon phase. Perhaps you are working on a love theme; you might want to add six hearts, six flowers, and six gemstones on your altar with your manifesting or freedom list, mirror, and candle. The coordinating Tarot card can be used as a visual activation. Flowers, colors, and gemstones accent your intentions. The fragrance provides a special connection to Spirit. You may want to burn candles of this scent, spritz your aura or your altar with the fragrance, or simply sniff the fragrance to awaken your olfactory system. Go to www.beatrex.com for moon mists, mirrors, and candle wraps.

"I" Statements

These statements align the Self with the characteristics of the astrological sign and the house the sign lives in.

Body – Mind – Spirit

Each astrological sign rules a body part, a mental trait or attitude, and a spiritual condition. This section is provided to increase understanding of the tendencies and patterns that are activated during the moon transit.

The Elements

Each moon cycle has a primary element (earth, air, fire or water), attached to the astrological sign to which it is assigned, that brings you more awareness of what to work on during the cycle.

Dropping Moon

This happens when a new or full moon peaks at the same time as it goes void. During a "dropping moon" it becomes very important for you to write your manifesting or your freedom list about half an hour before the designated time.

Choice Points: Light – Shadow – Wisdom

Dimensional Astrology presents us with a prescribed action for each of the 360-degrees on the astrology wheel. The object of Dimensional Astrology is to depolarize and neutralize. Each degree for the Moon are described to better enhance your understanding of the phase and its effects on you and your world. The wisdom comes when we experience and combine the light and the shadow without judgment.

Sabian Symbols

Each degree in the chart is identified with a symbolic language that speaks to your unconscious awareness and leads you to a new potential. The Sabian Symbols were given birth in California in 1925 by Mark Edmond Jones, a noted astrologer, with gifted clairvoyant Elsie Wheeler.

House Themes

Each house the Moon moves through brings a focus for that moon as a baseline for self-development during the moon phase.

Karmic Awakenings

Every once in a while the chart for the Moon will show an intercepted astrological sign in a house on the chart. This indicates that a karmic pattern is in operation on that day.

Clearing the Slate

The first step to accepting freedom is to clear the slate from trigger points that need to be released as we head into the full moon cycle. Each section is filled with trigger points that are specific to the astrological sign where the Moon resides. See if any of them feel familiar. Acknowledge what's familiar and then follow the instructions by writing down what happened and perform Ho'oponopono, the Hawaiian forgiveness ritual. For example, a negative trigger point for Leo is impatience. When you find yourself being impatient, write down the circumstances or journal about it. Then, looking in the mirror, apologize to yourself, ask for forgiveness, have gratitude for yourself with thanks that you could see your impatience as a trigger, and then return to love.

Victories and Challenges

These are sets of affirmations designed to say out loud during a specific moon cycle to determine a motivational tone for your self-discovery. After saying all of them out loud, you will know which statement applies to you. Circle the one that is yours and use it as a personal mantra daily during the moon phase.

Gratitude List

Keep this list active throughout this cycle. This will bring you to a level of completion so that a new cycle of opportunity can occur in your life.

Freedom List

Where do you feel the need to be free?

Victory List

Acknowledge what you have overcome. Keep this list active throughout this cycle. Honoring victories allows you to accept success.

Manifesting List

Write down what you want to create and manifest in your life.

List Ideas

Use these ideas to jump start your own lists. Let your imagination take off from here.

Sky Power Yoga

After manifesting, setting yourself free, and recalibrating by facing your trigger points, and after becoming open to being victorious, yoga allows the body to hold the position for manifesting or for freedom.

Please consult your doctor if you need to determine whether yoga exercises are suitable for you. If a pose is contraindicated for you, energetic benefit can still be obtained by envisioning the steps rather than doing them physically. Otherwise, proceed from a modified stance that has been medically-approved for you.

Before following any advice or practice suggested by this book, it is recommended that you consult your doctor as to its suitability, especially if you suffer from any health problems or special conditions. The publishers, the author, and associates cannot accept responsibility for any injuries or damage incurred as a result of following the exercises in this book, or using any of the therapeutic methods described or mentioned.

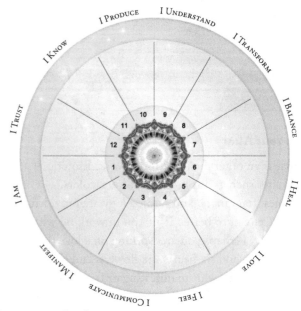

The Astro Wheel

Western astrological charts are placed within a circle or wheel. The wheel is a picture of the sky from a particular place and time on Earth. It is divided into 12 parts called "houses." Each house deals with a particular area of life. Key concepts for each house are written outside the wheel. Compare the wheel in the book to your very own chart and discover the theme that you will be living personally during the moon phase. (See table on page 14)

You will want to use a natal chart for yourself that clearly shows the degrees and the houses. For the preferred chart to use with this book, visit www.beatrex.com and look for the link to download a free chart. You will need to know the date, time, and place of your birth.

Cosmic Check-In

"I" statements are designed specifically to keep you in touch with all of the signs and their houses each time the Moon is new or full. Fill in the blanks to complete each statement during each full and new moon phase to activate all parts of your birth chart and keep you in touch with Oneness. Have fun noticing how different you are during each cycle.

Blank Pages

Between each moon phase blank pages are provided for journaling.

Tibetan Numerology of the Day

2	**Balance**	Be decisive and move past vacillation.
3	**Fun**	Have a party. Take on a creative project. Express the "Disneyland" side of yourself.
4	**Structure**	Take the day to organize. Get the job done. Work and you will sail through the day.
5	**Action, exercise, travel**	Exercise—join a gym, take a dance class, play tennis, go for a walk. Travel—go for a drive, travel the world, visit your travel agent. Make a change.
6	**Love**	Go out for a night of romance. Work on beauty in your home. Nurture yourself and take care of your health.
7	**Research**	Read a book. Learn something new and get smart. Take a class.
8	**Money**	Have a business meeting. Meet with your accountant. Make a sales call. Start a new business.
9	**Connecting with the Divine**	Meditate. Take part in a humanitarian project. Do community service.
10	**Seeing the "big picture"**	Take an innovative idea and run with it today!
11	**Completion**	Do what it takes to be complete.

Color Glossary

●	**Red**	Passion, bloodline, circulation, ancestry
●	**Pink**	Shy passion, learning to stand up for yourself, unconditional love, timid, colors in between the vertebrae of the spinal cord teaching you to stand up yourself
●	**Orange**	Money, sex, power, creativity, Christ healer, integration of the physical at a deeper level
●	**Yellow**	Enlightenment, a bright mind (perhaps too logical), happiness, joy, playful, higher mind, purist form of logic, the Sun
●	**Green**	Natural, nature, envy, abundance, heart, go
●	**Turquoise**	Sky power, spontaneous, futuristic, innovative
●	**Blue**	Third-eye perception, moody, water, the flow of emotion, depth, psychic, fantasy, throat, communication, emotional body
●	**Indigo**	Absence of guilt, opening to aspects of the future, creating new pathways
●	**Violet**	Magical thinking, abstract thinking, abstract mind, guilt-ridden
●	**Purple**	Ego, royalty, controlling version of power
●	**Rainbow**	Indicates a good future, open to all possibilities
●	**Gold**	Personal value, self worth, valuable
●	**Silver**	Intuition, reflective, ability to see yourself, the Moon
○	**White**	Major change, includes all colors
●	**Clear**	Clarity, cleaning, getting it clear, no color
●	**Black**	Intuitive, receptive, emptiness, absence of color, inner self, the void

Heavenly Bodies

☉	Sun	Outer personality, potential, director, the most obvious traits of the consciousness projection
☽	Moon	Emotion, feelings, memory, unconsciousness, mother's influence, ancestors, home life
☿	Mercury	The way you think, the intention beneath your thoughts, communication, academia (lower mind)
♀	Venus	Beauty, value, romantic love, sensuality, creativity, being social, fun, femininity
♂	Mars	Action, change, variety, sex drive, ambition, warrior, ego, athletics, masculinity
♃	Jupiter	Benevolent, jovial, excessive, expansive, optimistic, abundant, extravagant, accepting good fortune
♄	Saturn	Teacher, karma, disciplined, restrictive, father's influence
♅	Uranus	Liberated, revolutionary, explosive, spontaneous, breakthrough, innovation, technology
♆	Neptune	Mystical, charming, sensitive, addictive, glamorous, deceptive, illusions
♇	Pluto	Money, wealth, transformation, secrets, hidden information, sexuality, psychic power
⚷	Chiron	Wounded healer, healing, holistic therapies
☊	North Node	This represents where you are headed in this lifetime. In other words, it represents the direction your life will take you, your future focus. In Eastern astrology, this is sometimes called the "head of the dragon."
☋	South Node	This represents what you brought with you this lifetime and what you are moving away from. It is sometimes called the "tail of the dragon" in Eastern astrology.

The Astro Wheel

		Statement	Ruling Sign		Key Notes
1st House		**I Am**	♈	Aries	Your outer appearance, the way you present yourself, the way you dress, the way you enter a room, and what you leave behind when you leave the room.
2nd House		**I Manifest**	♉	Taurus	The way you make your money and the way you spend your money.
3rd House		**I Communicate**	♊	Gemini	How you get the word out and the message behind the words.
4th House		**I Feel**	♋	Cancer	The way your early environmental training was and how that set your foundation for living, and why you chose your mother.
5th House		**I Love**	♌	Leo	The way you love and how you want to be loved.
6th House		**I Heal**	♍	Virgo	The way you manage your body and its appearance.
7th House		**I Balance**	♎	Libra	One-on-one relationships, defines your people attraction, and how you work in relationships with the people you attract.
8th House		**I Transform**	♏	Scorpio	How you share money and other resources, what you keep hidden regarding sex, death, real estate, and regeneration.
9th House		**I Understand**	♐	Sagittarius	The way you approach spirituality, philosophy, journeys, higher knowledge, and aspiration.
10th House		**I Produce**	♑	Capricorn	Your approach to status, career, honor, and prestige, and why you chose your Father.
11th House		**I Know**	♒	Aquarius	Your approach to friends, social consciousness, teamwork, community service, and the future.
12th House		**I Trust**	♓	Pisces	Determines how you deal with your karma, unconscious software, and what you will experience in order to attain mastery by completing your karma. It is also about the way you connect to the Divine.

Astrological Signs

Each sign of astrology has a particular quality or tone that is described in more detail with the moons.

Sign	"I" Statement		Element	Key Words
♈ Aries	I Am	Sign of the Ram Ruled by Mars ♂ Begins the zodiac year with the Spring Equinox	Fire	Ego, identity, championship, leadership, action-oriented, warrior, and self-first.
♉ Taurus	I Manifest	Sign of the Bull Ruled by Venus ♀	Earth	Self-value, abundant, aesthetic, business, sensuous, art, beauty, flowers, gardens, collector, and shopper.
♊ Gemini	I Communicate	Sign of the Twins Ruled by Mercury ☿	Air	Versatile, expressive, restless, travel-minded, short trips, flirt, gossip, "nose for news," and the messenger.
♋ Cancer	I Feel	Sign of the Crab Ruled by the Moon ☽ Begins with the Summer Solstice	Water	Emotional, nurturing, family-oriented, home, mother, cooking, security-minded, ancestors, builder of form and foundation.
♌ Leo	I Love	Sign of the Lion Ruled by the Sun ☉	Fire	Willful, dramatic, loyal, children, child-ego state, love affairs, decadent, royal, show-stopper, theatre, adored and adoring.
♍ Virgo	I Heal	Sign of the Virgin Ruled by Mercury ☿	Earth	Gives birth to Divinity, perfectionist, discernment, scientific, analytical, habitual, work-oriented, body maintenance, earth connection, attention to detail, service-oriented, earth healer, herbs, and judgmental.
♎ Libra	I Balance	Sign of the Scales Ruled by Venus ♀ Begins with the Autumnal Equinox	Air	Relationship, social, harmony, industry, the law, diplomacy, morality, beauty, strategist, logical, and over-active mind.
♏ Scorpio	I Transform	Sign of the Scorpion Ruled by Pluto ♀ and Mars ♂	Water	Intense, passionate, sexual, powerful, focused, controlling, deep, driven, and secretive.
♐ Sagittarius	I Understand	Sign of the Archer Ruled by Jupiter ♃	Fire	Optimistic, generous, preacher-teacher, world traveler, higher knowledge, goal-oriented, philosophy, culture, publishing, extravagance, excessive, exaggerator, and good fortune.
♑ Capricorn	I Produce	Sign of the Goat Ruled by Saturn ♄ Begins at the Winter Solstice	Earth	Ambitious, concretive, responsible, achievement, business, corporate structure, world systems, and useful.
♒ Aquarius	I Know	Sign of the Water Bearer Ruled by Uranus ♅	Air	Inventive, idealistic, utopian, rebellion, innovative, technology, community, friends, synergy, group consciousness, science, magic, trendy, and future-orientation.
♓ Pisces	I Trust	Sign of the Fishes Ruled by Neptune ♆	Water	Sensitive, creative, empathetic, theatre, addiction, escape artist, glamor, secretive, Divinely guided, healer, medicine.

January

January 1: Full Moon in Cancer

This brings us to a space where the cosmic architects come alive and take a 'clean sweep' approach to our inner space and remove what is not in our best interest. It is time for our light to recalibrate to the new energy and illuminate us from the inside out.

January 1-2, 28-29: Low Vitality

The Earth is at a low physicality. Take extra care of yourself. Do not over extend your energy, take naps instead.

January 1 - March 25: Mars and Jupiter coupled in Scorpio

Expect a large amount of energy to boost your sensual self. Bring it on! If focused properly you can expect to have a huge amount of energy to take on any project. Market it towards an audience that will provide a wide-ranging success factor.

January 2: Uranus goes direct in Aries

This illuminates the idea of freedom and opens the pathway for the peaceful warrior to be birthed and actualize. Now is the time!

January 10: Mercury enters Capricorn

Thinking becomes practical.

Jan 10-11: Super Sensitivity

Keep your energy close to yourself. Slow down. Avoid travel if possible. Avoid trying to overcome. Chaos can get the better of you if you let it.

January 16: New Moon in Capricorn

Time to manifest a new plan for success. Remember to write your wish list and accept your victories.

January 17: Venus enters Aquarius

A need to experience a new kind of love happens suddenly. Have fun and stay committed to be uncommitted.

January 19: Sun moves into Aquarius

Get involved with a group that is making a difference by being in service to the future. Create your team and go for it.

January 26: Mars enters Sagittarius

This is motivating an adventure into the depths of the unknown.

January 31: Mercury enters Aquarius

This creates an opening in the mind to think beyond academia.

January 31: Full Moon in Leo – Blue Moon – Lunar Eclipse

Yikes! Where were you 19 years ago? Anything you have that is still attached to you from 1999 will be removed. Be willing to set yourself free. Let nature take care of you.

January 31: North Node conjunct Venus

Love comes in a new and different package and may not be recognizable.

January 31: South Node conjunct Moon

There is a tendency here to revert back to old feminine ways. Don't let the traditions of the past trap you.

Sunday	Monday	Tuesday	Wednesday	Thursday	Friday	Saturday
	1 ♅ S℞ ▼ New Year's Day ○ 11°♋38' – 6:24 PM ☽→♋ 12:10 AM 4. Build a solid foundation.	**2** ▼ ☽-V/C 2:46 PM ☽→♌ 11:22 PM ♅ SD 24°♈34'- 6:12 AM 5. Make changes willingly.	**3** 6. Make healthy choices.	**4** ☽-V/C 3:09 PM 7. Study something new.	**5** ☽→♍ 12:12 AM 8. Enjoy your abundance.	**6** ☽-V/C 6:50 PM 9. Be open to spiritual blessings.
7 ☽→♎ 4:14 AM 10. Bring on a new beginning.	**8** 2. Find your point of balance.	**9** ☽-V/C 8:12 AM ☽→♏ 12:05 PM 3. Live what you believe.	**10** ▲ ☿→♑ 9:10 PM 4. A practical solution is available.	**11** ▲ ☽-V/C 6:53 AM ☽→♐ 11:04 PM 5. Try a new approach.	**12** 6. Make your home loving.	**13** 7. Read something new.
14 ▲ ☽-V/C 12:47 AM ☽→♑ 11:42 AM 8. Share your wealth.	**15** ▲ Martin Luther King 9. Come from a loving heart.	**16** ● 26°♑54'–6:17 PM ☽-V/C 10:29 PM 10. The past is obsolete.	**17** ☽→♒ 12:31 AM ♀→♒ 5:45 PM 11. Embrace Universal Truth.	**18** 3. Live from experience.	**19** ☽-V/C 3:51 AM ☽→♓ 12:26 PM ☉→♒ 7:10 PM 4. Connect all the pieces.	**20** 5. Choose a different route.
21 ☽-V/C 5:21 PM ☽→♈ 10:26 PM 6. Beautify your home.	**22** 7. Learn from another.	**23** ☽-V/C 8:15 PM 8. Celebrate others' success.	**24** ☽→♉ 5:39 AM 9. Offer your services to a senior in need.	**25** ☽-V/C 7:16 PM 10. See a bright tomorrow.	**26** ☽→♊ 9:39 AM ♂→♐ 4:57 AM 11. You can have it all.	**27** 3. Believe in your dreams.
28 ▼ ☽-V/C 2:39 AM ☽→♋ 10:57 AM 4. All the parts count.	**29** ▼ 5. Enjoy a variety of opportunities.	**30** ☽-V/C 8:40 AM ☽→♌ 10:52 AM 6. Have flowers in the house.	**31** ○→11°♌37' 5:26AM Lunar Eclipse 5:29AM ☿→♒ 5:40 AM 7. Read an enlightening book.			

♈ Aries	♍ Virgo	♓ Pisces	♃ Jupiter	→ Enters	2. Balance	8. Money
♉ Taurus	♎ Libra	☉ Sun	♄ Saturn	℞ Retrograde	3. Fun	9. Spirituality
♊ Gemini	♏ Scorpio	☽ Moon	♅ Uranus	S/D Stationary Direct	4. Structure	10. Visionary
♋ Cancer	♐ Sagittarius	☿ Mercury	♆ Neptune	V/C Void-of-Course	5. Action	11. Completion
♌ Leo	♑ Capricorn	♀ Venus	♇ Pluto	▲ Super Sensitivity	6. Love	
	♒ Aquarius	♂ Mars	⚷ Chiron	▼ Low Vitality	7. Learning	

Full Moon in Cancer

When the Sun is Opposite the Moon

Full moons are always in opposition to the Sun. This creates a feeling of tension between where you want to shine and how your feelings are flowing on a sensory level about the Sun's directive. The two forces seem like they are working against each other, yet they are on the same team displaying different techniques to obtain the same mission. The Cancer/Capricorn polarity creates tension between being at home with your family or being at work positioning yourself for success.

Cancer Goddess

Birds are the symbol of expanded consciousness because they are born twice; once into the egg and once out of the egg. They are associated with rebirth and self-realization. Bird Woman is the Cancer goddess. She teaches us that, although we live in the illusion that security comes from our identity in the outer world, our true cosmic significance must be found within. Bird Woman directs us toward discovering our way home to our Soul, the place of lotus light. She has the ability to fly between Heaven and Earth, bringing communications from the angels and the spirit guides. She inspires souls to infuse matter with light—the true essence of co-creating.

Build Your Altar

Colors   Shades of gray and milky, creamy colors

Numerology   4 – Build a solid foundation

Tarot Card   The Chariot – The ability to move forward

Gemstones   Pearl, moonstone, ruby

Plant Remedy   Shooting Star – The ability to move straight ahead

Fragrance   Peppermint – The essence of the Great Mother

Moon Notes

January 1st, 6:24 PM

Full Moon   11° Cancer 38'
   Full Moons are about releasing, letting go, becoming free, and recalibrating.

Statement   I Feel

Body   Breast and stomach

Mind   Worry, self-pity

Spirit   Nurturing

Element
   Water – Taking the path of least resistance, going with the flow, creativity at its best. Secretive, glamourous, sensual, psychic, magnetic, actress, escape artist, and healer.

Choice Points
   Light   Recognizing greatness
   Shadow   Precocious
   Wisdom   Your emotional responses are fuel for other entities.

Sabian Symbol
   A Chinese woman nursing a baby whose aura reveals him to be the reincarnation of a great teacher.

Potential
   Open yourself to a message of hope, and remember to nurture your wisdom.

12th House Moon   I Trust/I Feel

Umbrella Energy
   The hidden awareness comes to the light to experience what you forgot to learn from your last life. Time to master a forgotten part of yourself.

Karmic Awakening
   Gemini/Sagittarius – Illuminating the polarity between Knowing and Thinking, and knowing the difference between academia and cosmic intelligence.

Clearing the Slate

Sixty hours before the full moon, negative traits connected to the astro-sign might become activated to trigger what needs to be released during the full moon phase. You may notice an unusual amount of worry, moodiness, addiction to the past, or challenges related to the energy of mothering. Make a list, look in the mirror, and for each negative trait, tell yourself *I am sorry, I forgive you, thank you for your awareness,* and *I love you.*

Cancer Victories & Challenges

Say all of the statements in this section out loud. Then, underline the phrase that means the most to you. Use the phrase as your affirmation for recalibrating throughout this moon phase.

Today, I take advantage of my ability to take action and position myself for success. I clearly know that the road to success is before me, and all I need to do is move forward. I am aware that when I take action and move forward, the Universe fills in the dots. Whether I move left, right, or straight ahead doesn't matter—what matters is that I am in movement. Today, I release indecisiveness that keeps me stuck. Today, I let go of vacillation that exhausts my mind. Today, I take my foot off of the brakes and find the gas pedal. I allow movement to occur, even if I don't know where I am going. When I take action, I trust the guideposts will appear. I am aware that action leads me to my new direction. Today, I know and GO! I remember that Karma comes to the space of non-action, while success comes through action. Action brings me to my victory. Standing still leads to regret, resentment, and chaos. I am aware that action can be as simple as taking a walk on the beach, buying fresh flowers to add a new dimension to my home, or simply going to a new restaurant for lunch. I take action today to break up a crystallized pattern and, in so doing, my life begins to show me newfound awareness and light to guide me.

Cancer Homework

It's now time to conquer pride and ambition, overcome fear of loneliness, release the need for money, security, and possessions, discover the value of emotions, and connect to beauty. Submerge yourself in a tub of water, relax, and let the clean water flow through your cells to wash away all of your hurts, resentments, and history that keep you trapped in the past. Pull the plug and let the spiral of water carry away your pain. Be prepared to boldly claim your presence in the present. Look around your kitchen and throw away the pots and pans that continue to feed your past, rather than vitalizing your life now.

Gratitude List

Keep this list active throughout the moon cycle. This will bring you to a level of completion so that a new cycle of opportunity can occur in your life. Be prepared for miracles!

Sky Power Yoga

Seated Cat/Cow

You need one chair for the prop.

With your back straight sit one hand-width from the back of the chair with your feet on the floor hip-width apart. If your feet require more solid contact with the floor, place pillows or folded towels under your feet.

Sit comfortably with a straight back and gently cup knees. Breathe in and out slowly and deeply several times through your nose with your awareness on your breasts.

Inhale and allow your belly to drop down as your pelvis tilts back into a subtle back bend.

As you inhale, say or think to yourself the mantra *I Feel*.

Exhale slowly as you tilt your pelvis forward and round your back slightly into a gentle forward bend while gazing down. Repeat with a smooth, continuous movement as many times as desired.

Freedom List

Say this statement out loud three times before writing your list:

I am a free spiritual being and it is my desire to be free to think and to express myself fully — to move about my life toward Truth and Wisdom — to accept and enjoy all good which is mine in living my truth.

Cancer Freedom Ideas

Now is the time to set myself free from self-pity, defensive behavior, nurturing everyone else but me, living in the past, being a mother, and having a mother.

I am now free and ready to make choices beyond survival!

Full Moon in Cancer

Your Personal Moon Experience

Fill in the Cosmic Check-In page. Then look up the degree of the Moon on the chart below. Take note of the "I" statement on the outside of the wheel where the Moon is located. Now, locate the same degree on your own chart and make

a note of the house and corresponding "I" statement. Go back to the Cosmic Check-In page, circle the two statements from the charts, and read what you wrote. This will give you an idea about what to expect from this moon phase on a personal level. For a personalized *My Moon Experience* Astrology reading with Beatrex, go to www.beatrex.com.

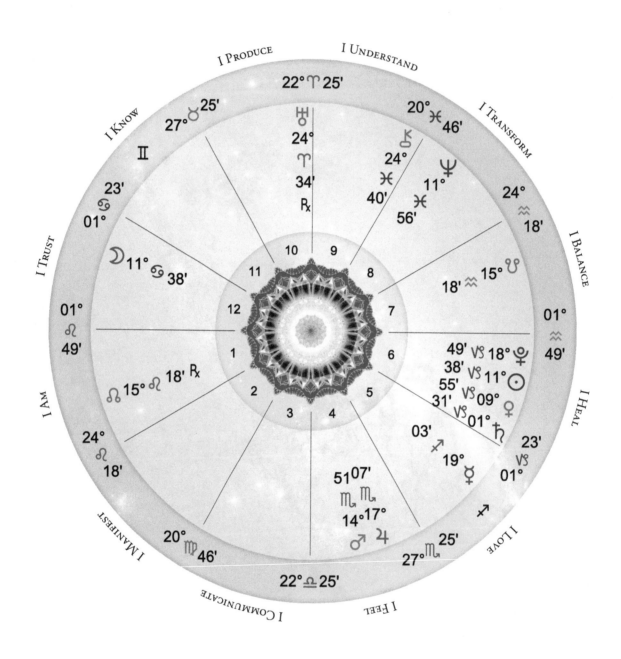

♈	Aries	♋	Cancer	♏	Scorpio	♓	Pisces
♉	Taurus	♌	Leo	♐	Sagittarius	☉	Sun
♊	Gemini	♍	Virgo	♑	Capricorn	☽	Moon
		♎	Libra	♒	Aquarius	☿	Mercury

♀	Venus	♅	Uranus	☊	North Node
♂	Mars	♆	Neptune	☋	South Node
♃	Jupiter	♇	Pluto	℞	Retrograde
♄	Saturn	⚷	Chiron		

Cosmic Check-in

Take a moment to write a brief phrase for each "I" statement.
This activates all areas of your life for this creative cycle.

♋ I Feel

♌ I Love

♍ I Heal

♎ I Balance

♏ I Transform

♐ I Understand

♑ I Produce

♒ I Know

♓ I Trust

♈ I Am

♉ I Manifest

♊ I Communicate

New Moon in Capricorn

When the Sun is in Capricorn

When the Sun is in Capricorn, we are given opportunities to receive the blessings of abundance and prosperity on a concrete level. Material satisfaction is at the top of the priority list for Capricorns. This is why they are known to be ambitious. Let integrity and goodwill set the standard for your recognition and accomplishments. Now is the time to take advantage of the energy by being useful and productive with a higher purpose. Capricorn is going through the most difficult times right now as the "old guard" is being swept away and creating space for the opening of the human heart. The presence of Pluto in this constellation is transforming all of the systems and structures that are so familiar and placing the Capricorn on unstable ground. Authority symbols and traditions are dissolving and opening new pathways for self-reliance to emerge as a reality, so that the idea of elitism can diminish and synergy will be the new status quo.

Capricorn Goddess

Srinmo, the ancestral Earth goddess of Tibet, holds "The Great Round" or "Wheel of Life" upon which all thoughts and deeds of humankind are recorded. She represents the wild, chaotic energy of the Feminine. Her incarnation in the land of Tibet is said to be held fast by twelve geomantic templates with Lhasa, the "plain of milk," representing her pulsing heart and life-giving breasts.

Carry a round object in your pocket between now and the full moon, to remind you of cycles and how Srinmo's karmic wheel brings your words, thoughts, and deeds back to you. Cycle a positive mantra in your mind to channel and harness your underground creative energy.

Build Your Altar

Colors	Forest green, tan, earth tones, deep red
Numerology	10 – The past is obsolete
Tarot Card	The Devil – Being a prisoner of a choice-less reality
Gemstones	Topaz, carnelian, amber, smoky quartz, jasper
Plant Remedy	Rosemary – The power of memory
Fragrance	Frankincense – Opens the gateway for the Soul to enter the body

Moon Notes

January 16th, 6:17 PM

New Moon 26° Capricorn 54'
New Moons are about manifestation, planting seeds, and becoming fruitful.

Statement	I Produce
Body	Knees
Mind	Authority issues
Spirit	Accepting success

Element
Earth – Practical, determined, structured, enduring, stubborn, traditional, stable, and stuck inside the box.

Choice Points
Light	Fidelity
Shadow	Superficiality
Wisdom	Accept the beauty of spirit to manifest love.

Sabian Symbol
A nature spirit dancing in the iridescent mist of a waterfall.

Potential
Unearthing the power of spirit in the illuminating light. Letting motion heal by combining earth, water, and air as a healing modality. Making essence manifest.

6th House Moon   I Heal/I Produce

Umbrella Energy
The concept of being of service is paramount here. Raising the standard of excellence, finding divinity in the details, working earth energy to heal and purify by going with nature, giving birth to Divinity, and practicing perfection without analyzation.

Capricorn Victories & Challenges

Say all of the statements in this section out loud. Then, underline the phrase that means the most to you. Use the phrase as your affirmation for recalibrating throughout this moon phase.

Ultimate fulfillment is mine today! My willingness to live my life to the fullest, each day, is making all of my dreams come true. I am fulfilling the promise of my destiny, and, in so doing, I make my mark on the world. I have completed my commitment to the Earth and to the cosmos by being all that I can be in the cycles of time on the inner and outer planes of awareness. All four seasons have been activated within me, so that I am in alignment and in motion with the cycles of releasing, rebirthing, planting, and harvesting. I can now claim my citizenship in all four worlds. I am open and ready for the inspiration that the spirit world brings me. I am ready to conquer the mental world by using thought, rather than thinking. I am open to the expression of my heart and the magnetic field of love that is ever-present in my experience. I am open to receive abundance from Nature and I contribute to the physical world by actively manifesting my ideas into reality. I am in harmony with the four elements and keep them active within me, as well as contribute to them externally. The element of air is within me as I breathe in the miracle of life. The element of earth is within me as I honor my body and use all of its senses to enhance the quality of life. I honor the Earth as my home and take complete stewardship of my home and property on this Earth. I honor the water, the wellspring of life eternal, and allow for the flow of my feelings and emotions to be a creative influence on the unconscious and conscious planes. I honor the fire within me as the spark of light that is a source of inspiration in my experience, and, in so doing, I have fulfilled the promise of my destiny to live fully, freely, and passionately on all levels and on all dimensions with my Earth-Cosmos connection.

Capricorn Homework

The Capricorn moon is the reincarnation of Spirit, emerging from the dark waters of our past emotions and releasing us from our fears of change and loss. Awaken your powerful and positive spiritual connection to be open to new possibilities. Ask yourself to move beyond your emotional loyalty to the past in order to manifest. We are reminded of our need for material and emotional security at this time. In order to insure this, we must learn to build a foundation for ourselves that is lit from within, and made from the materials of love, goodwill, and intelligence. Give yourself permission to throw away your watch and celebrate living in the moment.

Victory List

Acknowledge what you have overcome.
Keep this list active during this moon cycle.
Honoring victory allows you to accept success.

Sky Power Yoga

Standing Knee Circles

No props are needed.

Stand with your feet placed 4-6 inches apart with your legs straight and knees soft (not locked back). Place your hands on your hips and your gaze forward.

Close your eyes, and take several slow deep breaths in and out, through your nose. Inhale and exhale slowly, with presence. Breathe and settle into the pose before adding the mantra with the breath.

Inhale, standing tall with a long spine.

Pause and say or think to yourself the mantra, *I Produce*.

Bend at the knees and circle both knees in a

clockwise direction while exhaling slowly.

Inhale while coming back to the upright and straight-legged starting position for a pause. Repeat as many times as is comfortable.

Manifesting List

r

Capricorn Manifesting Ideas

Now is the time to focus on manifesting flexibility, productivity, authenticity, timing, new paradigms, transmuting, transformation, and re-translating structure.

This or something better than this comes to me in an easy and pleasurable way, for the good of all concerned. Thank you, Universe!

New Moon in Capricorn

Your Personal Moon Experience

Fill in the Cosmic Check-In page. Then look up the degree of the Moon on the chart below. Take note of the "I" statement on the outside of the wheel where the Moon is located. Now, locate the same degree on your own chart and make a note of the house and corresponding "I" statement. Go back to the Cosmic Check-In page and circle the two statements from the charts and read what you wrote. This will give you an idea about what to expect from this moon phase on a personal level. For more information on personalizing your *Moon Book*, go to www.BlueMoonAcademy.com and look for *How to Use the Moon Book*.

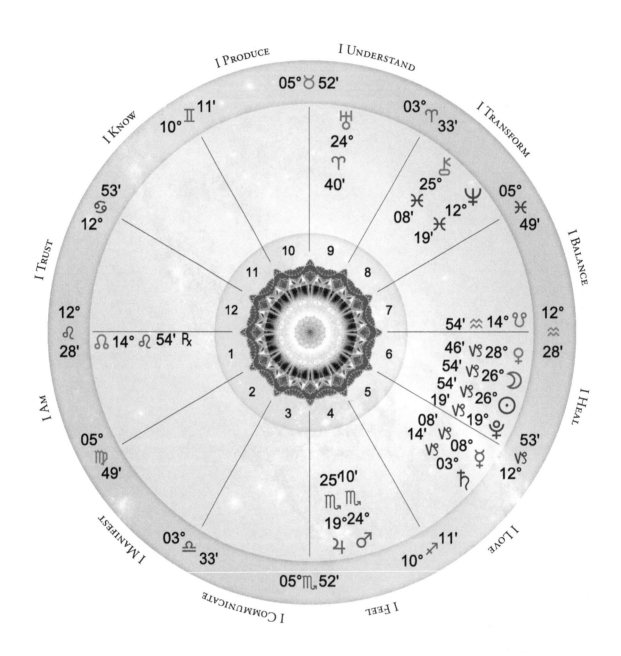

♈	Aries	♋	Cancer	
♉	Taurus	♌	Leo	
♊	Gemini	♍	Virgo	
		♎	Libra	

♏	Scorpio	♓	Pisces
♐	Sagittarius	☉	Sun
♑	Capricorn	☽	Moon
♒	Aquarius	☿	Mercury

♀	Venus
♂	Mars
♃	Jupiter
♄	Saturn

♅	Uranus
♆	Neptune
♇	Pluto
⚷	Chiron

☊	North Node
☋	South Node
℞	Retrograde

Cosmic Check-in

Capricorn New Moon
January 16th
6:17 PM

Take a moment to write a brief phrase for each "I" statement.
This activates all areas of your life for this creative cycle.

♑ I Produce

♒ I Know

♓ I Trust

♈ I Am

♉ I Manifest

♊ I Communicate

♋ I Feel

♌ I Love

♍ I Heal

♎ I Balance

♏ I Transform

♐ I Understand

Full Moon in Leo

When the Sun is Opposite the Moon

Full moons are always in opposition to the Sun. This creates a feeling of tension between where you want to shine and how your feelings are flowing on a sensory level about the Sun's directive. The two forces seem like they are working against each other, yet they are on the same team displaying different techniques to obtain the same mission. The Leo/Aquarius polarity creates tension about the need to be adored and the need to be free.

Leo Goddess

The depth of Winter is the dreaming time, when your seed has been planted. The colder temperatures and lack of light naturally draw us inside – within. Rhiannon, the Celtic Goddess, rides her horse through your dreams by night and guides your visions as you stare into the hearth fire. She transverses the liminal space, the doorway between the worlds.

Take a ride with Rhiannon, allowing her to transport you as you do your inner work. Revel in the silence of a quiet night before the fireplace. Find comfort in a hot cup of relaxing herbal tea. Rest and allow yourself a few extra hours of well-deserved sleep!

Build Your Altar

Colors	Royal purple, gold, orange
Numerology	7 – Read an enlightening book
Tarot Card	Strength – Passion for all of life
Gemstones	Amber, emerald, pyrite, citrine, yellow topaz
Plant Remedy	Sunflower – Standing tall in the center of life
Fragrance	Jasmine – Remembering your Soul's original intention

Moon Notes

January 31st, 5:26 AM
Lunar Eclipse

Full Moon 11° Leo 37'
Full Moons are about releasing, letting go, becoming free, and recalibrating.

Statement I Love

Body Heart and spinal cord

Mind Children, speculation

Spirit Love

Element
Fire – Igniting, dissolving, accelerating, cleansing, advancing awareness, impatience, leadership, passion, and vitality.

Choice Points
Light   Group relaxation
Shadow   Posturing
Wisdom   The intensity of energy available requires a buffer.

Sabian Symbol
An evening party of adults on a lawn illumined by fancy lanterns.

Potential
Taking a break from work, and relaxation with peers. Remember that it's important to give attention to your social life.

7th House Moon   I Balance/I Love

Umbrella Energy
When heart-to-heart connection happens. When partnership, marriage, working together, and living together happens. This is where the "we" in relating happens.

Karmic Awakening
Pisces/Virgo – Allopathic healing versus Nature healing.

Clearing the Slate

Sixty hours before the full moon negative traits connected to the astro-sign might become activated to trigger what needs to be released during the full moon phase. You may notice wanting an unusual amount of attention, resistance to authority, or strong impatience that expresses itself as a brat attack. Make a list, look in the mirror, and for each negative trait, tell yourself *I am sorry, I forgive you, thank you for your awareness,* and *I love you.*

Leo Victories & Challenges

Say all of the statements in this section out loud. Then, underline the phrase that means the most to you. Use the phrase as your affirmation for recalibrating throughout this moon phase.

I no longer feel the need to be in control and dominated by my mind telling me that it is appropriate to repress my feelings. I am going to claim my dominion today and feel the power of life running through me. I accept the privilege of being fully human and fully alive. I look to see where I lack courage to connect to what is natural for me. I see where I have been stubborn and turn to face my resistance. I become aware of when my higher self says "Go" and my lower self says "No." I am aware that my lower self (my body) is a creature of habit and will sabotage me with the idea that change takes too much energy. I take responsibility for the part of me that is a creature of habit and talk to my body about coming into alignment with my new intention to become fully passionate and fully alive. I remember today that in order to get the body to move forward with me, I need two-thirds of my cells to align with my request. First, I become aware of the part of myself that is trying to control all of my outcomes and keep me a slave to those outcomes, rather than trusting in the evolution of nature and the concept of Divine Order. I give up the fight today knowing that this struggle is dissipating all my energy and making me exhausted. In order for my body to respond, I need to awaken my cells through sound and touch. So, today I rub my body and speak out loud by sharing my request for connection, revitalization, rejuvenation, passion, and support. Today, I celebrate the idea that I can connect to my wholeness by activating my cells to support my commitment to my aliveness. I can now stand tall in the center of life and grow in self-confidence.

Leo Homework

Review your memorabilia and see what no longer matches your current love nature, your creative nature, and your loving self. Set your heart free while chanting, "Love is all you need." Become a part of the new consciousness on the Earth that brings a more abundant life when we expand the radius of our love. Live Love Every Day!

Gratitude List

Keep this list active throughout the moon cycle. This will bring you to a level of completion so that a new cycle of opportunity can occur in your life. Be prepared for miracles!

Sky Power Yoga

Reclined Heart Opener

You need two bath towels and one or two pillows for the prop.

Fold the two towels in half lengthwise, roll them into a log, and place them on the floor. Put both pillows on top of the rolled towels to support your back, neck, and head in the pose.

Sit on the floor with the support prop behind you.

Lean back onto your elbows and then lower back onto your support prop. This pose creates a gentle opening across your chest. If you find your head dangling over the top edge, shift your prop towards your head to support your head and neck fully.

Place your arms out at a 45-degree angle with palms facing upwards at your sides.

Relax. Close your eyes. Breathe in and out slowly and deeply several times through your nose keeping your awareness on your heart center. Allow your body to soften and relax.

Inhale deeply as you say or think to yourself the mantra *I Love.* Exhale slowly and relax fully into the support prop and the pose. Enjoy breathing with your mantra for a few minutes.

Freedom List

Say this statement out loud three times before writing your list:

*I am a free spiritual being and it is my desire to be free to think
and to express myself fully.*

Leo
Freedom Ideas

Now is the time to activate a game change in my life, and give up the need to be the center of attention, obstacles to generosity, false pride, false identity, blocks to confidence or creativity, excuses that keep me from quality time with my children, blocks to knowing that I am loved and lovable, and the idea that everyone needs to be devoted to me in all situations.

*From this day forward I resolve to be true – first to myself
and my highest self, and then to the highest self in me which
is the Source of Love That I Am.*

Full Moon in Leo

Your Personal Moon Experience

Fill in the Cosmic Check-In page. Then look up the degree of the Moon on the chart below. Take note of the "I" statement on the outside of the wheel where the Moon is located. Now, locate the same degree on your own chart and make

a note of the house and corresponding "I" statement. Go back to the Cosmic Check-In page, circle the two statements from the charts, and read what you wrote. This will give you an idea about what to expect from this moon phase on a personal level. For a personalized *My Moon Experience* Astrology reading with Beatrex, go to www.beatrex.com.

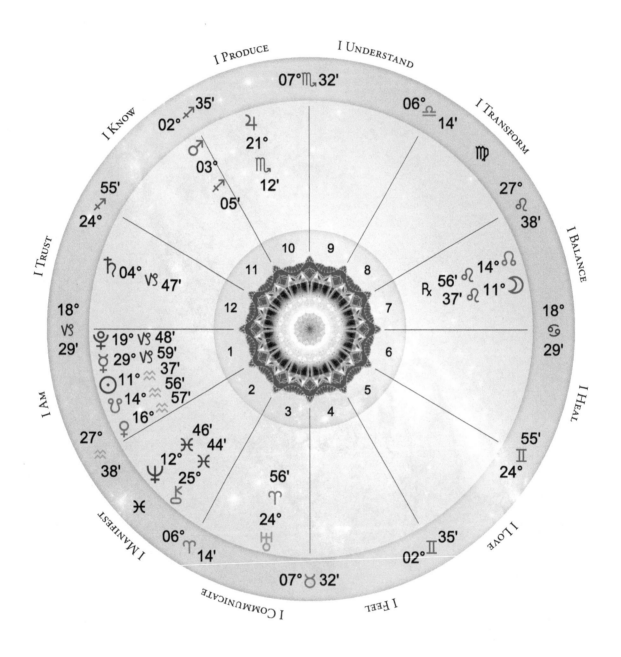

♈	Aries	♋	Cancer	♏	Scorpio	♓	Pisces	♀	Venus	♅	Uranus	☊	North Node
♉	Taurus	♌	Leo	♐	Sagittarius	☉	Sun	♂	Mars	♆	Neptune	☋	South Node
♊	Gemini	♍	Virgo	♑	Capricorn	☿	Mercury	♃	Jupiter	♇	Pluto	℞	Retrograde
		♎	Libra	♒	Aquarius	☽	Moon	♄	Saturn	⚷	Chiron		

Cosmic Check-in

Leo Full Moon
January 31st, 5:26 AM
Lunar Eclipse

Take a moment to write a brief phrase for each "I" statement.
This activates all areas of your life for this creative cycle.

♌ I Love

♍ I Heal

♎ I Balance

♏ I Transform

♐ I Understand

♑ I Produce

♒ I Know

♓ I Trust

♈ I Am

♉ I Manifest

♊ I Communicate

♋ I Feel

February

February 1 - March 25th Mars and Jupiter coupled in Scorpio

Expect a large amount of energy to boost your sensual self. Bring it on! If focused properly you can expect to have a great amount of energy to take on a huge project. Time to market your ideas toward an audience that will provide feedback with a wide range success.

February 10: Venus enters Pieces

The soul opens a doorway to romance. Expect depth and sincerity leading to a major connection. Beware of the realist taking over and destroying the illuminating bubble.

February 10-11: Super Sensitivity

Expect chaos, slow down, and keep your boundaries in check.

February 16: New Moon in Aquarius – Solar Eclipse – Chinese New Year

This is the Year of the Earth Dog, beginning Feb. 16, 2018, until Feb. 4, 2019. Dog is the eleventh in the 12-year cycle of the Chinese zodiac. Dog is 'our best friend' who understands the human's spirit and at the same time obeys its master, thus creating the idea of Mastery. Mastery asks us to take command of our situation and the dog carries this out without question. The Chinese consider the dog to be auspicious. If a dog happens to come to a house, it symbolizes the coming of fortune. Dogs teach loyalty, unconditional love, and protection. The directions that will be auspicious are South, Southeast, and East. Numbers that set the stage for good fortune are 3, 4, and 9. Opportunities come with ease when the colors green, red, purple are part of the process. Roses and cymbidium orchids assist in creating the right vibration for miracles to happen.

New Moon in Aquarius – Solar Eclipse

Time to set intentions for manifesting with the flavor of innovation. This eclipse is all about releasing us from any burdens that 1999 still holds.

February 17: Mercury enters Pisces

Your mental body becomes aware that an expanded view is necessary.

February 18: Sun enters Pisces

A deeper reality of Divine perfection comes forward to be processed and expanded.

February 24-25: Low Vitality

Time to take care of your physical body. Don't push, avoid resistance. Be willing to accept things as they are and rest well.

Sunday	Monday	Tuesday	Wednesday	Thursday	Friday	Saturday
				1 ☽-V/C 2:58 AM ☽→♍ 11:12 AM 8. Enhance your abundance.	**2** ☽-V/C 11:06 PM 9. The heart always knows.	**3** ☽→♎ 1:47 PM 10. Create a new way.
4 11. Know the Universal Truth.	**5** ☽-V/C 10:45 AM ☽→♏ 7:56 PM 3. Believe what you know.	**6** 4. Make the foundation real.	**7** ☽-V/C 11:16 PM 5. Take a different route.	**8** ☽→♐ 5:53 AM 6. Give a loving gift today.	**9** 7. Teach someone your wisdom.	**10▲** ☽-V/C 8:37 AM ☽→♑ 6:20 PM ♀→♓ 3:21 PM 8. Earn your own way to success.
11▲ 9. Forgive yourself.	**12** ☽-V/C 9:43 PM 10. Embrace transformation.	**13** ☽→♒ 7:11 AM 2. Decide then act.	**14** Valentine's Day 3. You are a creator.	**15** Chinese New Year ● 27°♒08' – 1:05 PM Solar Eclipse 27°♒07'–12:51 PM ☽-V/C 1:05 PM ☽→♓ 6:41 PM 4. Be a team player.	**16** 5. Change willingly.	**17** ☽-V/C 2:13 PM ♀→♓ 8:29 PM 6. Check your health.
18 ☽→♈ 4:04 AM ☉→♓ 9:19 AM 7. Analyze then act.	**19** President's Day 8. Share what you have.	**20** ☽-V/C 3:11 AM ☽→♉ 11:11 AM 9. Be emotionally supportive.	**21** 10. Accept the past is over.	**22** ☽-V/C 3:45 AM ☽→♊ 4:07 PM 2. Decide wisely.	**23** 3. What do you believe?	**24▼** ☽-V/C 11:57 AM ☽→♋ 7:05 PM 4. Face life squarely.
25▼ 5. Vary your choices.	**26** ☽-V/C 1:50 PM ☽→♌ 8:41 PM 6. Beauty adds dimension.	**27** 7. Think outside the box.	**28** ☽-V/C 3:13 PM ☽→♍ 9:57 PM 8. Be a leader who can follow.			

♈ Aries	♍ Virgo	♓ Pisces	♃ Jupiter	➡ Enters	2. Balance	8. Money
♉ Taurus	♎ Libra	☉ Sun	♄ Saturn	℞ Retrograde	3. Fun	9. Spirituality
♊ Gemini	♏ Scorpio	☽ Moon	♅ Uranus	℠ Stationary Direct	4. Structure	10. Visionary
♋ Cancer	♐ Sagittarius	☿ Mercury	♆ Neptune	V/C Void-of-Course	5. Action	11. Completion
♌ Leo	♑ Capricorn	♀ Venus	♇ Pluto	▲ Super Sensitivity	6. Love	
	♒ Aquarius	♂ Mars	⚷ Chiron	▼ Low Vitality	7. Learning	

New Moon in Aquarius

When the Sun is in Aquarius

This is a time when the higher octave of the mind comes into play and one is given the power of vision. The Aquarian energies promote knowing by being a wellspring of knowledge. They expand the radius of contact by going beyond the known in areas of communication and cooperation. Now is the time to be initiated into greater awareness to serve the fields of human endeavors. Connect and combine magic with science and become a creative influence. When the sun is in Aquarius we must unify with our team players and collect innovative ideas to advance the world to a better place.

Aquarius Goddess

White Tara steps in to assist you with compassionate acceptance and healing of old, deep wounds that are now illuminated by both the Sun and the Moon. With seven eyes (one on her forehead, one on each hand and each foot), White Tara's ability to see encompasses her ability to feel and connect with others and with the Earth. Her name is derived from the root "tri," which means to cross. She has accepted the task of remaining in feminine form until all beings are enlightened, and is here to help all cross the ocean of existence and suffering.

Call upon White Tara's guidance to navigate towards self-acceptance and self-forgiveness on your path to healing.

Build Your Altar

Colors	Violet, neon, crystalline rainbow tints
Numerology	4 – Be a team player
Tarot Card	The Star – Golden opportunities for the future
Gemstones	Aquamarine, blue topaz, peacock pearls
Plant Remedy	Queen of the Night Cactus – Ability to see light in the dark
Fragrance	Myrrh – Healing the nervous system

Moon Notes

February 15th, 1:05 PM
Solar Eclipse
Chinese New Year – Enter the Dog

New Moon 27° Aquarius 08'
New Moons are about manifestation, planting seeds, and becoming fruitful.

Statement	I Know
Body	Ankles
Mind	Genius
Spirit	Innovation

Element
Air – The breath of life that allows the mind to achieve new insights and fresh perspectives, inspiration, active and abstract dreaming, and freedom from attachments.

Dropping Moon
Write your intentions early, before the Moon goes void.

Choice Points
Light	Good in a crisis
Shadow	Lack of imagination
Wisdom	Exchange, transform and lead the way.

Sabian Symbol
An ancient pottery bowl filled with fresh violets.

Potential
Combining the ancient wisdom with the power of now to get your answer.

9th House Moon I Understand/I Know

Umbrella Energy
The way you approach spirituality, philosophy, journeys, higher knowledge, and aspiration.

Karmic Awakening
Sagittarius/Gemini – Higher knowledge versus academia.

Aquarius Victories & Challenges

Say all of the statements in this section out loud. Then, underline the phrase that means the most to you. Use the phrase as your affirmation for recalibrating throughout this moon phase.

Today, I chart my course for my new direction. My future is set on a new, fresh evolutionary course. I am guided by a higher source and trust in that guidance. I know my life has value and I am willing to contribute to the pool of consciousness by experiencing my life and living my life to the fullest view of possibility. Today, I know my possibilities are endless. My Spirit and my Soul are connected to Heaven and to Earth and this knowing brings me to the awareness that I can add to the higher qualities of life because I am connected to the whole. My being is far-reaching and immeasurable. I contribute to existence simply by knowing. All of the guideposts are connected for me today to see my way to a profound new future. My vision is clear and I can clearly set my sights on this new course. Golden opportunities come with this new vision and I trust in my guidance to bring me to this new level of manifesting power. I check in with my inner lights, each day, by meditating and asking for all seven of the energy centers in my body to come into alignment with the outer symbols of guidance. I do this by becoming still and breathing until I feel the stillness. Then, I place my hand on each center in my body, one center at a time, to be activated by light. Next, I ask out loud for each center in my body to let me know what its energetic contribution to the new direction is and how best to use the energy to move forward on my new course of action. I write down each statement and connect each statement to the guiding star in the sky. I am now linked up physically and spiritually and ready to navigate my total self towards my new evolutionary direction.

Aquarius Homework

Aquarians manifest a storehouse of information through innovative telecommunications, technology, social networking and media, and global communication. They are typically found in the fields of psychology, science fiction authoring or film-making, speech writing, and aerospace engineering.

Consider these three Aquarian gifts:

- Opportunity – Become a creative influence
- Enlightenment – When you become aware that you are light
- Brotherhood – Separation doesn't exist anymore

Where do you see these occurring in your life?

Victory List

Acknowledge what you have overcome.
Keep this list active during this moon cycle.
Honoring victory allows you to accept success.

Sky Power Yoga

Elevated Legs

You need two bath towels and one to two pillows for the prop.

Nest two towels together. Fold them lengthwise and roll into a log. Place the towel log on the floor and place your pillow on top for your support prop.

Sit on the floor with your legs straight in front of you and your feet hip-width apart. Place your prop between your feet and then place each foot on the prop.

Sit up straight. Lower yourself onto your elbows and then onto your back. Relax.

Close your eyes. Breathe in and out slowly and deeply several times through your nose with your awareness on your ankles.

Inhale. Say the mantra *I Know* either out loud or in your head.

Exhale softly and slowly. Enjoy breathing with your mantra for a few minutes.

Manifesting List

Aquarius Manifesting Ideas

Now is the time to focus on manifesting vision, invention, technology, freedom, friends, community, personal genius, higher awareness, teamwork, science, and magic.

This or something better than this comes to me in an easy and pleasurable way, for the good of all concerned. Thank you, Universe!

New Moon in Aquarius

Your Personal Moon Experience

Fill in the Cosmic Check-In page. Then look up the degree of the Moon on the chart below. Take note of the "I" statement on the outside of the wheel where the Moon is located. Now, locate the same degree on your own chart and make a note of the house and corresponding "I" statement. Go back to the Cosmic Check-In page and circle the two statements from the charts and read what you wrote. This will give you an idea about what to expect from this moon phase on a personal level. For more information on personalizing your *Moon Book*, go to www.BlueMoonAcademy.com and look for *How to Use the Moon Book*.

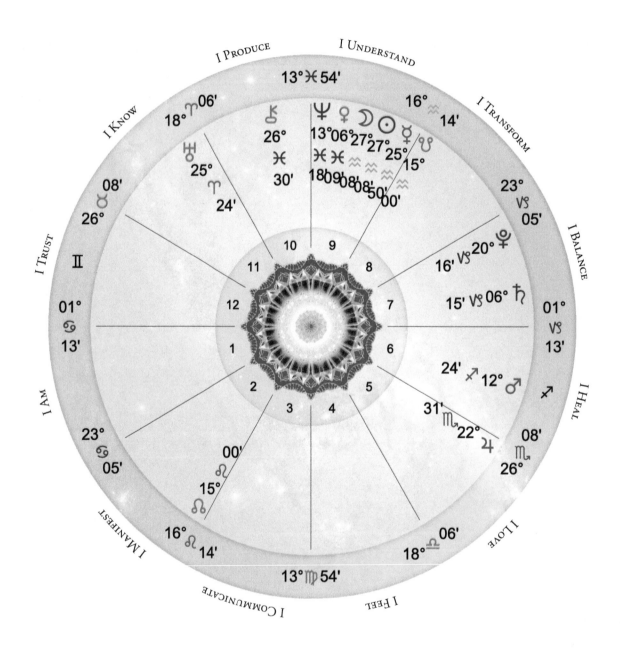

♈	Aries	♋	Cancer	♏	Scorpio	♓	Pisces	♀	Venus	♅	Uranus	☊	North Node
♉	Taurus	♌	Leo	♐	Sagittarius	☉	Sun	♂	Mars	♆	Neptune	☋	South Node
♊	Gemini	♍	Virgo	♑	Capricorn	☽	Moon	♃	Jupiter	♇	Pluto	℞	Retrograde
		♎	Libra	♒	Aquarius	☿	Mercury	♄	Saturn	⚷	Chiron		

Cosmic Check-in

Aquarius New Moon
February 15th, 1:05 PM
Solar Eclipse

Take a moment to write a brief phrase for each "I" statement.
This activates all areas of your life for this creative cycle.

♒ I Know

♓ I Trust

♈ I Am

♉ I Manifest

♊ I Communicate

♋ I Feel

♌ I Love

♍ I Heal

♎ I Balance

♏ I Transform

♐ I Understand

♑ I Produce

March

March 1: Full Moon in Virgo

Determine areas where space is not magnetizing to its optimum potential and recalibrate.

March 1: Chiron, Venus, and Mercury tripled in Pisces

This trifecta sets the stage for wounded women to heal.

March 5: Mercury enters Aries

Expect to do a lot of talking about yourself... it is time to express the true nature of your being. Highest thought should be considered when speaking.

March 6: Venus enters Aries

Expect an extra need for attention. Promote yourself in a graceful way. Remember that honey works better than vinegar. 'Brat attacks' are in the air if immediate gratification is not met.

March 8-9, 15-17: Super Sensitivity

Rushing could create a lot of chaos and bring on regret. Be mindful and deliberate with your actions.

March 8: Jupiter retrograde in Scorpio until July 10

Watch out for an exaggerated version of investigation, it could get you in trouble. Expect a bit of smoke and mirrors around being visible. It is time to go below the radar and stand in the background for awhile.

March 17: Mars enters Capricorn

Order and structure becomes interesting at this time. A more subtle approach to life will come into play. Your fiery expression and passionate enthusiasm will appear to be enhanced by mood... 'If you are cold you are cold, if you are hot you are hot.'

March 17: New Moon in Pisces

Time to meditate with a group and realize your spiritual connection. The deepest part of your soul wants company, now is the time to merge with a new perspective.

March 20: Sun enters Aries – Spring Equinox

We are now awakened into our true connection with the very essence of this year. The Equinox will set the stage to manifest this year's spiritual purpose. Let it Be!

March 22: Mercury retrograde in Aries until April 15

The key to being successful during this retrograde is to slow down. Going fast at this time will lead to dysfunction of some sort and could hurt.

March 24-25: Low Vitality

Stamina is a challenge right now. Let yourself find a place to rest and feel calm. The Earth is fragile. Don't waste energy by being resistant to this. Let 'new' rule.

March 30: Venus enters Taurus

May all your days be auspicious during this transit. This is a great time for comfort and pleasure. Enjoy life to the fullest. Shopping is good. Parties will be the best. Let yourself dance on the table tops!

March 31: Full Moon in Libra – Blue Moon

This is a reminder that the emotional, creative, and feeling side of the brain needs to accept its power. TIME TO STAND UP FOR YOURSELF!

March 31: Mars and Saturn conjunct in Capricorn

You will be feeling suppressed, repressed, and/or limited. When you step forward you will have to do it again... "one step forward, two steps back." Avoid travel, if possible.

March 31: Uranus and Venus conjunct in Taurus

This opens a field of awareness for the feminine to be re-defined. The Earth presents us with an unexpected way to take Stewardship. Time to make adjustments and accept this new approach.

Sunday	Monday	Tuesday	Wednesday	Thursday	Friday	Saturday
				1 ○11°♍23′ - 4:51 PM 9. Feel the emotion.	2 ☽-V/C 3:50 PM 10. Make a fresh start.	3 ☽→♎ 12:20 AM 2. Review your options.
4 ☽-V/C 10:18 PM 3. Relax and be creative.	5 ☽→♏ 5:22 AM ☿→♈ 11:35 PM 4. Make the platform secure.	6 ♀→♈ 3:47 PM 5. There are other choices.	7 ☽-V/C 12:54 AM ☽→♐ 2:02 PM 6. Let others help out.	8 ♃℞ ▲ ♃S℞-23°♏13′ - 8:47 PM 7. Think it through.	9 ♃℞ ▲ ☽-V/C 6:27 PM 8. Make life more enjoyable.	10 ♃℞ ☽→♑ 1:51 AM 9. Pray for success.
11 ♃℞ PDT Begins 10. Live in the now.	12 ♃℞ ☽-V/C 8:35 AM ☽→♒ 3:44 PM 2. Gather opinions then act.	13 ♃℞ 3. A joyful heart wins.	14 ♃℞ 4. Patience is your friend.	15 ♃℞ ▲ ☽-V/C 12:32 AM ☽→♓ 3:11 AM 6. Beauty empowers our actions.	16 ♃℞ ▲ 7. Experiences make you wise.	17 ♃℞ ▲ St. Patrick's Day ●26°♓53 - 6:11 AM ☽-V/C 6:11 AM ☽→♈ 11:56 AM ♂→♑ 9:41 AM 8. Fill your cup with more.
18 ♃℞ 9. Let your heart speak.	19 ♃℞ ☽-V/C 12:29 PM ☽→♉ 6:06 PM 10. Make tomorrow count.	20 ♃℞ Spring Equinox ☉→♈ 9:17 AM 2. Let harmony unfold.	21 ♃℞ ☽-V/C 10:20 AM ☽→♊ 10:29 PM 3. Create what you require.	22 ☿♃℞ ☿S℞-16°♈53′ - 5:20 PM 4. All team members count.	23 ☿♃℞ ☽-V/C 8:52 PM 5. Advance beyond resistance.	24 ☿♃℞ ▼ ☽→♋ 1:52 AM 6. Prepare for romance.
25 ☿♃℞ ▼ ☽-V/C 11:57 PM 7. Get a larger view.	26 ☿♃℞ ☽→♌ 4:44 AM 8. Give prosperity a chance.	27 ☿♃℞ 9. Serve your high ideals.	28 ☿♃℞ ☽-V/C 2:54 AM ☽→♍ 7:30 AM 10. Follow your light, it knows where to go.	29 ☿♃℞ ▼ ☽-V/C 9:58 PM 2. Think and then decide.	30 ☿♃℞ ▼ ☽→♎ 10:51 AM ♀→♉ 9:55 PM 3. Put on your party shoes.	31 ☿♃℞ Passover ○10°♎45′ - 5:36 AM 4. Organize the mess.

♈ Aries	♍ Virgo	♓ Pisces	♃ Jupiter	→ Enters	2. Balance	8. Money
♉ Taurus	♎ Libra	☉ Sun	♄ Saturn	℞ Retrograde	3. Fun	9. Spirituality
♊ Gemini	♏ Scorpio	☽ Moon	♅ Uranus	S/D Stationary Direct	4. Structure	10. Visionary
♋ Cancer	♐ Sagittarius	☿ Mercury	♆ Neptune	V/C Void-of-Course	5. Action	11. Completion
♌ Leo	♑ Capricorn	♀ Venus	♇ Pluto	▲ Super Sensitivity	6. Love	
	♒ Aquarius	♂ Mars	⚷ Chiron	▼ Low Vitality	7. Learning	

Full Moon in Virgo

When the Sun is Opposite the Moon

Full moons are always in opposition to the Sun. This creates a feeling of tension between where you want to shine and how your feelings are flowing on a sensory level about the Sun's directive. The two forces seem like they are working against each other, yet they are on the same team displaying different techniques to obtain the same mission. The Virgo/Pisces polarity creates tension between doing your work and finding your path.

Virgo Goddess

Astraea is the virgin Goddess of Purity, who fled the Earth upon seeing weaponry, warfare, and the rise of patriarchy that destroyed the earth goddess culture during the Iron Age. She ascended to the heavens to become the constellation Virgo, to watch over the Earth until she will one day return issuing in a new Utopian age. Often depicted as a star maiden, she has wings and a shining halo or crown of stars, and carries a flaming torch or thunderbolt.

Ask Astraea to help you as you sort through the details to bring love and light into a fresh new perspective, free from the restrictions of the past. "Because it's always been done that way," is no longer a viable excuse. Sharing what you love, with the intention for the highest and best for all, enlists Astraea's blessings.

Build Your Altar

Colors	Green, blue, earth tones
Numerology	9 – Feel the emotion
Tarot Card	The Hermit – Knowing your purpose and sharing it with the world
Gemstones	Emerald, sapphire
Plant remedy	Sage – The ability to hold and store light
Fragrance	Lavender – Management and storage of energy

Moon Notes

March 1st, 4:51 PM

Full Moon 11° Virgo 23'
   Full Moons are about releasing, letting go, becoming free, and recalibrating.

Statement	I Heal
Body	Intestines
Mind	Critical
Spirit	Divinity is in the details.

Element
   Earth – Practical, determined, structured, enduring, stubborn, traditional, stable, and stuck inside the box.

Choice Points
Light	Inspired ambition
Shadow	Ambiguous
Wisdom	Curiosity leads you to new discoveries.

Sabian Symbol
   A bride with her veil snatched away.

Potential
   Show your true face in any situation, you will no longer be able to hide behind a veil.

1st House Moon I Am/I Heal

Umbrella Energy
   Your outer appearance, the way you present yourself, the way you dress, the way you enter a room, and what you leave behind when you leave the room.

Karmic Awakening
   Gemini/Sagittarius – Challenges between higher knowledge and academia.

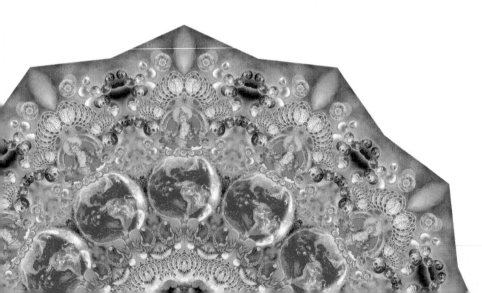

Clearing the Slate

Sixty hours before the full moon, negative traits connected to the astro-sign might become activated to trigger what needs to be released during the full moon phase. You may notice an extreme sense of judgement, an obsession for detail, or letting perfectionism stop your action. Make a list, look in the mirror, and for each negative trait, tell yourself *I am sorry, I forgive you, thank you for your awareness,* and *I love you.*

Virgo Victories & Challenges

Say all of the statements in this section out loud. Then, underline the phrase that means the most to you. Use the phrase as your affirmation for recalibrating throughout this moon phase.

Today I take time to go within to be silent. I imagine myself on a country road moving towards a beautiful mountain. I bask in the glory of the power of the mountain and know that it is calling me to the top. I find a pathway to the top and begin to climb. As I climb I become aware of a presence guiding me and empowering me to keep going, creating a sense of peacefulness within me.

I become aware of my own power in this silent journey to the top and revel in the serenity that nature and silence bring me. At last I am about to reach the summit and, just before I do, I feel the power drawing me to go within on a deeper level. I stop for a moment and look back at the path I have just climbed and know that my life's path is a remarkable gift. I connect to the center of the Earth and feel an inner glow.

The top of the mountain calls to me and, as I reach the top, a voice says to me, "Take in the view and look in all directions." As I turn 360-degrees, I sense a light igniting me in every direction. Then the voice says, "Look up!" Now, my awareness shifts and I see that I have become an illuminating light glowing in all six directions. Next I hear, "Sit in your silence and take in the vastness of who you are. Who you are is immeasurable." I sit, feeling the glow of light within me, and become aware of a greater plan for my life. I allow myself to receive this plan. I accept this assignment and slowly walk down the mountain, knowing that I can be a shining light for myself and others. I know I must take my light out to the world and share what I know to be my truth. Today, I become a messenger for the light.

Virgo Homework

Become integrated so that the light of your personality becomes soul-infused. When you are soul-infused and are in service to your Higher Self, you radiate love and light through the power of the inner self through all activities, thoughts, and emotions and become more magnificent. Learn the art of detachment and let your Soul take control.

Gratitude List

Keep this list active throughout the moon cycle. This will bring you to a level of completion so that a new cycle of opportunity can occur in your life. Be prepared for miracles!

Sky Power Yoga

Prone Spinal Twist

You need two bath towels and one pillow for the prop.

Nest the two towels, fold in half lengthwise, and roll them into a log. Place the towel log on the floor with the pillow on top for your support prop.

Sit on your side with your right hip on the floor. Place your support prop at a 90-degree angle to your thigh.

Inhale anchoring your sitting bones to the floor and lengthening your spine. Exhale and gently lower your upper torso down onto the prop. Your gaze is the same direction as your knees. This creates a subtle restorative twist. Walk your hands forward in order to release your shoulders.

Relax. Close your eyes. Breathe in and out slowly and deeply several times through your nose with your awareness on your intestines.

Inhale deeply as you say or think to yourself the mantra *I Heal*.

Exhale slowly and relax more deeply into the pose.

Breathe with your mantra for a few minutes before repeating on the opposite side.

Freedom List

Say this statement out loud three times before writing your list:

I am a free spiritual being and it is my desire to be free to think and to express myself fully.

Virgo
Recalibrating Ideas

Now is the time to activate a game change in my life, and give up finding fault with myself, my addiction to perfection, my addiction to detail, over-indulging in image management, pain-producing thinking patterns, judgment of others, resistance to being healthy, and destructive behaviors.

I hereby fully and completely free my mind from all adhesions to outdated philosophies, habits, relationships, groups of people, man-made laws, moral codes, all rules, set ideas and set ways of thinking, traditions, organizations, duty-motivated activities, guilt, judgment, and being misunderstood!

Full Moon in Virgo

Your Personal Moon Experience

Fill in the Cosmic Check-In page. Then look up the degree of the Moon on the chart below. Take note of the "I" statement on the outside of the wheel where the Moon is located. Now, locate the same degree on your own chart and make

a note of the house and corresponding "I" statement. Go back to the Cosmic Check-In page, circle the two statements from the charts, and read what you wrote. This will give you an idea about what to expect from this moon phase on a personal level. For a personalized *My Moon Experience* Astrology reading with Beatrex, go to www.beatrex.com.

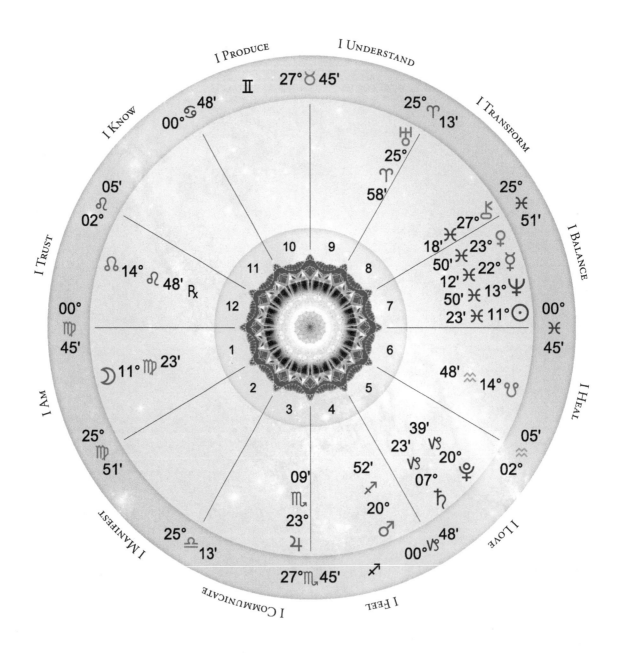

♈	Aries	♋	Cancer	♏	Scorpio	♓	Pisces	♀	Venus	♅	Uranus	☊	North Node
♉	Taurus	♌	Leo	♐	Sagittarius	☉	Sun	♂	Mars	♆	Neptune	☋	South Node
♊	Gemini	♍	Virgo	♑	Capricorn	☽	Moon	♃	Jupiter	♇	Pluto	℞	Retrograde
		♎	Libra	♒	Aquarius	☿	Mercury	♄	Saturn	⚷	Chiron		

Cosmic Check-in

Virgo Full Moon
March 1st
4:51 PM

Take a moment to write a brief phrase for each "I" statement.
This activates all areas of your life for this creative cycle.

♍ I Heal

♎ I Balance

♏ I Transform

♐ I Understand

♑ I Produce

♒ I Know

♓ I Trust

♈ I Am

♉ I Manifest

♊ I Communicate

♋ I Feel

♌ I Love

New Moon in Pisces

When the Sun is in Pisces

This is a time when you come in contact with your most Divine essence. It is a time to meditate and connect to your higher purpose. Let your intuition guide you to a program of service. Let your Soul take control and connect to a space beyond your ego. In order to do this, you must become free of your habits, hang ups, and fantasies. Compassion frees you from the slavery of self-interest and the lure of your personality's blind urges, emotional traps, and mental crystallizations. When the Soul takes control, you unite your personality with Divine essence and radiate the light needed to find your true pathway.

Pisces Goddess

This new moon, Canola, the Irish mistress of the harp, tugs at your heartstrings. In myth, Canola took a walk after quarrelling with her lover one night, and fell asleep outdoors to hypnotic music. The next morning she awoke to find that it was the sound of the wind passing through the sinews of a whale carcass; from this she invented the harp.

Trust the messages that come to you through song. Take a break to breathe, chant, and sing to your heart's content, knowing that the sound will carry your will and intention, with beauty, harmony, and balance, into the world, healing yourself and others. Bring the spring plants to life with your voice!

Build Your Altar

Colors	Turquoise, blue, green, aqua
Numerology	8 – Fill your cup with more
Tarot Card	The Moon – The inner journey, reflection, illumination
Gemstones	Amethyst, opal, jade, turquoise
Plant Remedy	Passion flower – The ability to live in the here and now
Fragrance	Lotus – Connecting to the Divine without arrogance

Moon Notes

March 17th, 6:11 AM

New Moon 26° Pisces 53'
  New Moons are about manifestation, planting seeds, and becoming fruitful.

Statement	I Trust
Body	Feet
Mind	Super-sensitive
Spirit	Mystical

Element
  Water – Taking the path of least resistance, going with the flow, creativity at it's best. Secretive, glamourous, sensual, psychic, magnetic, actress, escape artist, and healer.

Dropping Moon
  Write your intentions early, before the Moon goes void.

Choice Points
  Light   Self-discipline
  Shadow   Denial
  Wisdom Coordinate your thoughts, they are all part of the puzzle.

Sabian Symbol
  Watching the very thin moon crescent appearing at sunset, different people realize that the time has come to go ahead with their different projects.

Potential
  Applying your talents in new directions.

1st House Moon I Am/I Trust

Umbrella Energy
  Your outer appearance, the way you present yourself, the way you dress, the way you enter a room, and what you leave behind when you leave the room.

Pisces Victories & Challenges

Say all of the statements in this section out loud. Then, under-line the phrase that means the most to you. Use the phrase as your affirmation for recalibrating throughout this moon phase.

I see my path clearly now. I know I must walk by myself on this journey into the deepest part of my Soul. It is time to clear the way and look beneath the surface to discover the parts of myself that I have placed in the unconscious world to be worked on at a later date. That later date is now. I am aware that the postponement of my inner reality can no longer be delayed.

Evolution is pulling me and it has become greater than my distractions, my fear, my denial, and my refusal to face what I have hidden from myself and others. I am aware of outside influences that pull me away from facing my inner realms. I know, without a doubt, that I am only as sick as the secrets I keep from myself and others. I see clearly how these distractions, illusions, and secrets need to be recognized so I can find the separated parts of myself that have been left in the dark, obscured from the light. I know that it is time to bring myself into wholeness and bring my shadow side to the light of my awareness.

I begin by closing my eyes and experiencing darkness. I imagine walking on a lonely road, in the dark, by myself. I pay particular attention to the sensations in my body and allow for the body to guide me to the places of dullness, numbness, fear, and anxiety. I simply allow for the intelligence of the body to coordinate the feeling with an image, person, or an event. I stay still and know, from the depth of my being, that recognition is all that is required of me right now. When recognition occurs, the light of awareness is ignited and the conscious world will take care of the rest. I know that the road to enlightenment requires me to first take the road into the dark side of my Soul.

Pisces Homework

Pisces manifest by using their psychic powers for counseling, therapy, hypnosis, the ministry, and creating spiritual schools or healing centers. They are also successful in visionary arts, acting, music, medical and pharmaceutical fields, and oceanography.

Take time to go within to discover where new pathways are open for advancement. Blessings pour forth to those who move toward these pathways in the spirit of service. Be open to these pathways and consider the ones that benefit our planet with new ideas, creative expression, and expanded views that lead people to higher levels of service.

Victory List

Acknowledge what you have overcome.
Keep this list active during this moon cycle.
Honoring victory allows you to accept success.

Sky Power Yoga

Seated Foot Flex

You need one chair for the prop.

With a straight back sit in a chair with your feet on the floor hip-width apart. Feet should have solid contact with the floor. Use pillows or folded towels to support your feet, if necessary.

Bring your right foot forward.

Relax. Close your eyes. Breathe in and out slowly and deeply several times through your nose with your awareness on your feet.

Point your right toe. Inhale deeply. Say the mantra *I Trust* either out loud or in your head. Then pause and lift only your toes.

Exhale and flex your whole foot.

Relax and breathe. Repeat three times and change legs.

Manifesting List

Pisces Manifesting Ideas

Now is the time to focus on manifesting connection with the Divine, creativity, healing powers, psychic abilities, sensitivity, compassion, and service.

This or something better than this comes to me in an easy and pleasurable way, for the good of all concerned. Thank you, Universe!

New Moon in Pisces

Your Personal Moon Experience

Fill in the Cosmic Check-In page. Then look up the degree of the Moon on the chart below. Take note of the "I" statement on the outside of the wheel where the Moon is located. Now, locate the same degree on your own chart and make a note of the house and corresponding "I" statement. Go back to the Cosmic Check-In page and circle the two statements from the charts and read what you wrote. This will give you an idea about what to expect from this moon phase on a personal level. For more information on personalizing your *Moon Book*, go to www.BlueMoonAcademy.com and look for *How to Use the Moon Book*.

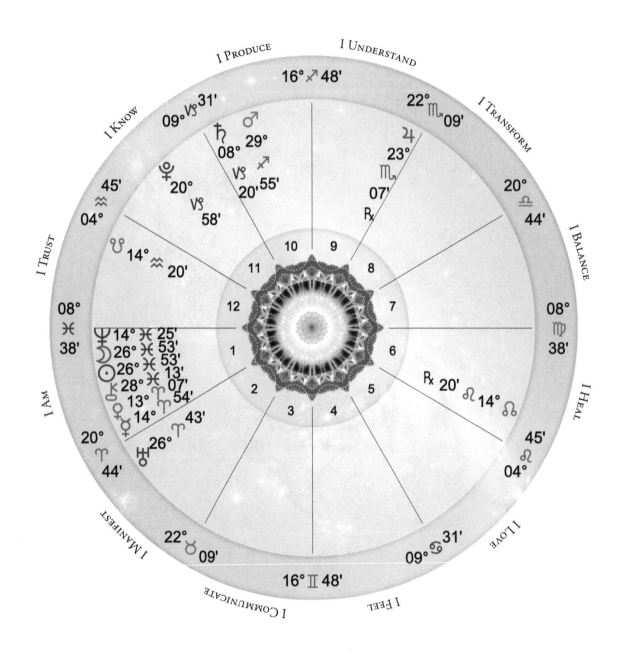

♈	Aries	♋	Cancer	♏	Scorpio	♓ Pisces
♉	Taurus	♌	Leo	♐	Sagittarius	☉ Sun
♊	Gemini	♍	Virgo	♑	Capricorn	☿ Mercury
		♎	Libra	♒	Aquarius	

♀ Venus	♅ Uranus	☊ North Node
♂ Mars	♆ Neptune	☋ South Node
♃ Jupiter	♇ Pluto	℞ Retrograde
♄ Saturn	⚷ Chiron	

Cosmic Check-in

Pisces New Moon
March 17th
6:11 AM

Take a moment to write a brief phrase for each "I" statement.
This activates all areas of your life for this creative cycle.

♓ I Trust

♈ I Am

♉ I Manifest

♊ I Communicate

♋ I Feel

♌ I Love

♍ I Heal

♎ I Balance

♏ I Transform

♐ I Understand

♑ I Produce

♒ I Know

Full Moon in Libra

When the Sun is Opposite the Moon

Full moons are always in opposition to the Sun. This creates a feeling of tension between where you want to shine and how your feelings are flowing on a sensory level about the Sun's directive. The two forces seem like they are working against each other, yet they are on the same team displaying different techniques to obtain the same mission. The Libra/Aries polarity creates tension between the idea of "We" versus "Me."

Libra Goddess

Ostara, Goddess of the Spring Equinox, walks into your life creating a carpet of fragrant flowers in her wake with each step upon the Earth. Freed from the ice and snow of Winter, she bathes in the moonlight and breathes out warmer breezes to turn up the temperatures. This moon is the harbinger, a rebirth of the Earth to fresh growth and abundance.

What is blooming new in your life? What do your seeds need to shed and break through to bask in the bright Spring sunlight? Take Ostara's blessing of jasmine or rose fragrance into the bath or shower and allow the warm water to wash away the old.

Build Your Altar

Colors	Pink, green
Numerology	4 – Organize the mess
Tarot Card	Justice – The ability to stay in the center of polarity
Gemstones	Rose quartz, jade
Plant remedy	Olive trees – Stamina
Fragrance	Eucalyptus – Clarity of breath

Moon Notes

March 31st, 5:36 AM

Full Moon 10° Libra 45'
Full Moons are about releasing, letting go, becoming free, and recalibrating.

Statement	I Balance
Body	Kidneys
Mind	Social
Spirit	Peace

Element
Air – The breath of life that allows the mind to achieve new insights and fresh perspectives, inspiration, active and abstract dreaming, and freedom from attachments.

Choice Points
Light	Flexible focus
Shadow	Extremes
Wisdom	See all sides of a situation. Gather other opinions and then decide.

Sabian Symbol
Miners are surfacing from a deep coal mine.

Potential
A subconscious healing coming to the light.

7th House Moon I Balance/I Balance

Umbrella Energy
One-on-one relationships. Libra defines your people attraction, and how you work in one-on-one relationships with the people you attract.

Clearing the Slate

Sixty hours before the full moon negative traits connected to the astro-sign might become activated to trigger what needs to be released during the full moon phase. You may notice an unusual need to defend, an over-shadowing guilt, or a need to justify. Make a list, look in the mirror, and for each negative trait, tell yourself *I am sorry, I forgive you, thank you for your awareness,* and *I love you.*

Libra Victories & Challenges

Say all of the statements in this section out loud. Then, underline the phrase that means the most to you. Use the phrase as your affirmation for recalibrating throughout this moon phase.

I am awakened to the reality of the Law of Cause and Effect. I take time out today to see what is coming back to me. I know my actions, my words, and my thoughts have life and manifest in a pattern that returns to me. Today, I am in a place where I can clearly see the results of my words, my actions, and my thoughts. I am aware that it is time for a review and, in so doing, I am given the opportunity to balance, integrate and redistribute these results in a more productive way. When I truly know and experience the Law of Cause and Effect (what I send out comes back to me), I can take responsibility for my actions, words, and thoughts, and set myself free of blame. When blame is gone from my thought pattern (self-inflicted or circumstantial), I am able to benefit from my review rather than wasting energy justifying or defending my position. I now accept the idea that I am free to reconcile with whatever I have labeled as an injustice in my life. I take the time to re-route my thinking towards making life a beneficial experience. Today, I accept that in changing my language I can change my life. Today, I prepare to take actions toward beneficial experiences. Today, I release the need to be right and accept the right to be. Today, I stop judging life and start living life.

Libra Homework

Let the fresh air blow away mental stagnation related to times when you let others' interests supersede your own. Drink an excess amount of water to alert your kidneys that the recalibration process has commenced. It's time to deepen your intention to be one with the light, promoting restoration on Earth.

Gratitude List

Keep this list active throughout the moon cycle. This will bring you to a level of completion so that a new cycle of opportunity can occur in your life. Be prepared for miracles!

Sky Power Yoga

Elevated Legs

You need two bath towels and one to two pillows for the prop.

Nest two towels together. Fold them lengthwise and roll into a log. Place the towel log on the floor and place your pillow on top for your support prop.

Sit on the floor with your legs straight in front of you and your feet hip-width apart.

Place your prop between your feet and then place each foot on the prop.

Sit up straight. Lower yourself onto your elbows and then onto your back. Relax. Close your eyes. Breathe in and out slowly and deeply several times through your nose with your awareness on your kidneys.

Inhale deeply. Say the mantra *I Balance* either out loud or in your head. Exhale slowly. Enjoy breathing with your mantra for a few minutes in this relaxing and rejuvenating pose.

Freedom List

Say this statement out loud three times before writing your list:

I am a free spiritual being and it is my desire to be free to think and to express myself fully.

Libra
Recalibrating Ideas

Now is the time to activate a game change in my life, and give up situations that are not balanced, people-pleasing and the need to be liked, sorrow over past relationships, unsupportive relationships, the need to be right, false accusations, and being misunderstood.

I hereby fully and completely free my mind from all adhesions to outdated philosophies, habits, relationships, groups of people, man-made laws, moral codes, all rules, set ideas and set ways of thinking, traditions, organizations, duty-motivated activities, guilt, judgment, and being misunderstood!

Full Moon in Libra

Your Personal Moon Experience

Fill in the Cosmic Check-In page. Then look up the degree of the Moon on the chart below. Take note of the "I" statement on the outside of the wheel where the Moon is located. Now, locate the same degree on your own chart and make a note of the house and corresponding "I" statement. Go back to the Cosmic Check-In page, circle the two statements from the charts, and read what you wrote. This will give you an idea about what to expect from this moon phase on a personal level. For a personalized *My Moon Experience* Astrology reading with Beatrex, go to www.beatrex.com.

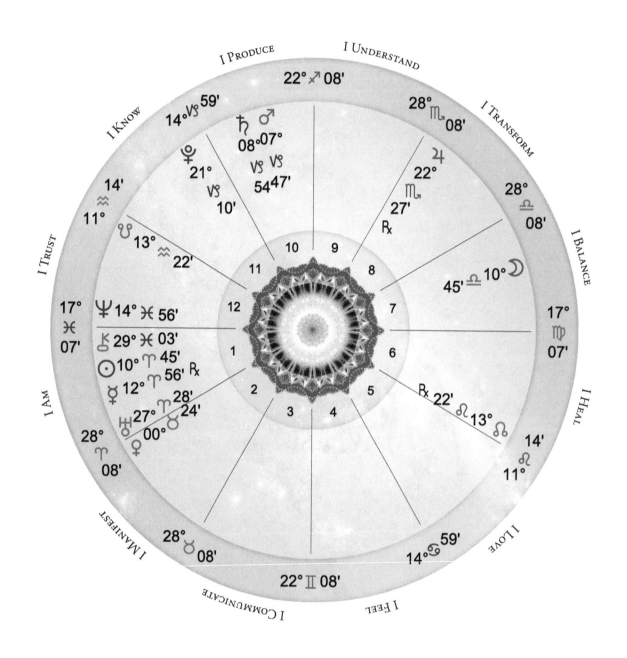

♈	Aries	♋	Cancer	♏	Scorpio	♓	Pisces	♀	Venus	♅	Uranus	☊	North Node
♉	Taurus	♌	Leo	♐	Sagittarius	☉	Sun	♂	Mars	♆	Neptune	☋	South Node
♊	Gemini	♍	Virgo	♑	Capricorn	☽	Moon	♃	Jupiter	♇	Pluto	℞	Retrograde
		♎	Libra	♒	Aquarius	☿	Mercury	♄	Saturn	⚷	Chiron		

Cosmic Check-in

Libra Full Moon
March 31st
5:36 AM

Take a moment to write a brief phrase for each "I" statement.
This activates all areas of your life for this creative cycle.

♎ I Balance

♏ I Transform

♐ I Understand

♑ I Produce

♒ I Know

♓ I Trust

♈ I Am

♉ I Manifest

♊ I Communicate

♋ I Feel

♌ I Love

♍ I Heal

April

April 6-7: Super Sensitivity

The concept of order seems to have left the planet and outside influences are shaky. Trying to fix things right now could lead to a disaster. Let it be!

April 15-29: Pluto and Mars in Capricorn

The ego is in trouble and is fighting for 'top dog' position. This is one fight that must be released! Accept the invitation to use 6th-dimensional power which involves taking the high road and using your ability to let go. If not, second-dimensional power will take over and brut force could create verbal and/or physical injuries you might regret.

April 15: Sun, Uranus, and the Moon tripled in Aries

This could be very explosive if you tend to be emotional. Your potential could find a niche to grow from. Bliss could add to the quality of your expression.

April 15: Mercury goes direct in Aries

Advancement can happen now. Putting yourself first makes victory a reality. Accept the edge of victory being yours now without bragging. Yes! You are a winner.

April 17: Saturn retrograde until September 6

Time to remember that knowledge is experience. Look at the events in your life and honor what you have learned from them. Saturn is a happy influence when you honor what life is teaching you.

April 17: Chiron enters Aries

This is a landmark 'Soul Code' moment! The wounded healer moves out of the vastness of healing your relationship with God, and moves into the 'Central Self' for an up-close-and-personal look at your ego. Time to heal your righteousness and move into love. Remember your ego wants to be right and your consciousness wants to live love.

April 19: Sun enters Taurus

Time to manifest. You're able to make it happen now because you know you are valuable.

April 20-21: Low Vitality

Learn the power of letting go by using recalibration to detach. Expand – Supersede – and Include.

April 22: Pluto retrograde in Capricorn until September 30

Take on a research project to make the best use of this transit. Time to re-establish a knowing of how money works, and set up new foundations for manifestation.

April 24: Venus enters Gemini

Time to flirt and have a blast.

April 29: Saturn, Pluto, and Mars, tripled in Capricorn

Expect a battle of the ego to occur. The desire to be 'top dog' is very strong here and competition is in fierce operation. Be aware and don't take it too seriously.

Sunday	Monday	Tuesday	Wednesday	Thursday	Friday	Saturday
1 ☿♃℞ Easter ☽-V/C 11:29 AM ☽→♏ 3:57 PM 5. Modify a redundant task.	**2** ☿♃℞ 6. Flowers bring peace to your home.	**3** ☿♃℞ ☽-V/C 9:05 AM ☽→♐ 11:54 PM 7. Think and listen for the answer.	**4** ☿♃℞ 8. Make money your friend.	**5** ☿♃℞ 9. Learn a mantra.	**6** ☿♃℞ ▲ ☽-V/C 6:35 AM ☽→♑ 11:01 AM 10. Realize the beginning starts now.	**7** ☿♃℞ ▲ 11. Embrace the Universal vision.
8 ☿♃℞ ☽-V/C 7:39 PM ☽→♒ 11:50 PM 3. Joy is living in the moment.	**9** ☿♃℞ 4. Be a team player.	**10** ☿♃℞ 5. What peaks your curiosity today?	**11** ☿♃℞ ☽-V/C 7:55 AM ☽→♓ 11:39 AM 6. Healthy actions bring quick results.	**12** ☿♃℞ 7. Use wisdom, the solution is apparent.	**13** ☿♃℞ ☽-V/C 4:27 AM ☽→♈ 8:25 PM 8. Honor success, celebrate victories.	**14** ☿♃℞ 9. Let your spirit soar.
15 ♃℞ ● 26°♈02′ - 6:57 PM ☽-V/C 10:59 PM ☿S/D-4°♈46′-2:22 AM 10. The future is full of magic.	**16** ♃℞ ☽→♉ 1:50 AM 2. Look for more than three options.	**17** ♄♃℞ ☽-V/C 3:04 PM ♄S/R-9°♑9′-6:48 PM ⚷→♈ 1:09 AM 3. Use creativity to stimulate projects.	**18** ♄♃℞ ☽→♊ 5:02 AM 4. Use all the tools in your toolbox.	**19** ♄♃℞ ☉→♉ 8:14 PM 5. Find different paths to a solution.	**20** ♄♃℞ ▼ ☽-V/C 5:04 AM ☽→♋ 7:26 AM 6. Watch your health.	**21** ♄♃℞ ▼ 7. More analysis may help.
22 ♄♃♇℞ ☽-V/C 7:57 AM ☽→♌ 10:08 AM ♇S/R-21°♑17″-8:23 AM 8. Pray for abundance for everyone.	**23** ♄♃♇℞ 9. Be of service to the high road.	**24** ♄♃♇℞ ☽-V/C 11:39 AM ☽→♍ 1:40 PM ♀→♊ 9:41 AM 10. Begin anew each day.	**25** ♄♃♇℞ 2. Honor the harmony within.	**26** ♄♃♇℞ ☽-V/C 2:49 AM ☽→♎ 6:12 PM 3. Always be your creative self.	**27** ♄♃♇℞ 4. Have a firm structure.	**28** ♄♃♇℞ ☽-V/C 10:31 PM 5. Change can be enjoyable.
29 ♄♃♇℞ ○ 9°♏39′ - 5:58 PM ☽→♏ 12:11 AM 6. Fill your day with love.	**30** ♄♃♇℞ ☽-V/C 7:56 PM 7. Discernment can bring new options.					

♈ Aries	♍ Virgo	♓ Pisces	♃ Jupiter	→ Enters	2. Balance	8. Money
♉ Taurus	♎ Libra	☉ Sun	♄ Saturn	℞ Retrograde	3. Fun	9. Spirituality
♊ Gemini	♏ Scorpio	☽ Moon	♅ Uranus	S/D Stationary Direct	4. Structure	10. Visionary
♋ Cancer	♐ Sagittarius	☿ Mercury	♆ Neptune	V/C Void-of-Course	5. Action	11. Completion
♌ Leo	♑ Capricorn	♀ Venus	♇ Pluto	▲ Super Sensitivity	6. Love	
	♒ Aquarius	♂ Mars	⚷ Chiron	▼ Low Vitality	7. Learning	

New Moon in Aries

When the Sun is in Aries

Aries awakens the dreamer from Winter sleep and represents the raw energy of Spring, when the new shoots of life burst forth. Aries is the fundamental, straightforward approach to life. There is no challenge that is too great, no obstacle too daunting, and no rival too powerful for the Aries. Aries symbolizes initiation, leadership, strength, and potency. Competition and achievement are very important to Aries. Now is the time to be a pioneer and break all barriers to become the winner you are.

Aries Goddess

Pandora was created by Zeus, who was angry about Prometheus stealing the secret of fire. She was the first human woman, whose name means "the all-giving." The gods all conspired to each invest her with seductive gifts. Hesiod's story tells us that Pandora's curiosity led her to open a jar (not a box) that unleashed evils upon humanity. However, Pandora, also known as Anesidora, "she who sends up gifts" from the Earth, could instead be interpreted as opening the pithos (the vessel), an ancient symbol of the Divine Feminine, and generously gifting the world with fertility and creativity.

As you reinterpret your identity this moon, ask Pandora to help you get curious and creative about the "I" you present to the world and how that contributes to the "We."

Build Your Altar

Colors	Red, black, white
Numerology	10 – The future is full of magic
Tarot Card	Emperor – Success on all levels
Gemstones	Diamond, red jasper, coral, obsidian
Plant Remedy	Pomegranates, oak – Planting new life and rooting new life
Fragrance	Ginger – The ability to ingest and digest life

Moon Notes

April 15th, 6:57 PM

New Moon 26° Aries 2'
New Moons are about manifestation, planting seeds, and becoming fruitful.

Statement	I Am
Body	Head
Mind	Impulsive
Spirit	Initiation

Element
Fire – Igniting, dissolving, accelerating, cleansing, advancing awareness, impatience, leadership, passion, and vitality.

Choice Points

Light	Recreate
Shadow	Retreat
Wisdom	Write your ideas. Get them out of your head to make room for other ideas!

Sabian Symbol
Through imagination a lost opportunity is regained.

Potential
Accepting a second chance.

7th House Moon I Balance/I Am

Umbrella Energy
One-on-one relationships. Libra defines your people attraction, and how you work in one-on-one relationships with the people you attract.

Aries Victories & Challenges

Say all of the statements in this section out loud. Then, underline the phrase that means the most to you. Use the phrase as your affirmation for recalibrating throughout this moon phase.

I am the author of my life. I accept that I am a winner and, in so doing, all doors are open to me. I hold the world in the palm of my hand and I know that there is not a mountain that I cannot climb. My ability to respond to life is in operation today and I direct my intention to bring me to the next level of self-determined achievement. The world and its systems are available for me to use as tools for my success and I use them with true excellence. I am organized and all systems are in place for me to make my mark on the world. I accept that my structured ground state and my dynamic energy are ready to make headway using pure determination, action, planning, and power. I will manage this plan and know that the sequence of events provided support me to make a breakthrough today.

I am willing to make my plan and take action on it. I gather my support team together today to focus on the appropriate action and encourage each person in their area of excellence and production. I am a great leader and my dynamic power is a good resource for others to determine their own success formula. I am aware that all parts of my team are important and place value on all areas of performance required to manifest in the world. I know how to place people in their best areas of expertise, so they can experience their own unique talent manifesting. Today, I honor my father for what he taught me by what he did, or didn't do, to encourage my ability to perform. I am the producer. I am the protector. I am the provider. I am the promoter. I am power. I am the author of my life.

Aries Homework

Aries manifest best through sales and promotions, and as a professional athlete, personal trainer or coach, martial arts expert, military professional, demolition expert, fireworks manufacturer, or wardrobe consultant.

Merge your light and dark forces so balance can occur. Then, give shape to your feelings through creative forms and learn to live in the duality of your Soul and watch your spirit soar! The embodiment of this duality connects you to the Unity, a requirement for these times.

Victory List

Acknowledge what you have overcome.
Keep this list active during this moon cycle.
Honoring victory allows you to accept success.

Sky Power Yoga

Mountain Pose

No props are needed.

Stand with your feet hip-width apart. Lift your toes, spread them wide, and place them back on the floor.

To massage the bottoms of your feet, rock back and forth and side to side for 30 seconds. Gradually make your movements more subtle until you find the sweet spot where your weight is balanced evenly across your feet.

Squeeze your thighs to lift your kneecaps. Slightly tuck your tailbone down and feel your hips align over your ankles.

Inhale, lengthening your spine. Exhale, rolling your shoulders back and down, reaching your fingertips towards the floor. Gently lift your chest from the sternum and turn your palms out slightly. Imagine a strong line of vertical energy running from the bottom of your feet to the top of your head.

Relax into the pose. Close your eyes. Breathe in and out

slowly and deeply several times through your nose with your awareness on your head.

Inhale deeply. Envision the energy of your breath coming up from the earth into your feet, up your legs, up your spine, and out the top of your head.

Say or think to yourself the mantra *I Am*. Exhale slowly. Envision the breath returning back into your head, down your spine, down your legs, out your feet and back into the earth. Repeat as desired.

Manifesting List

Aries
Manifesting Ideas

Now is the time to focus on manifesting personality power, leadership, strength, self-acceptance, winning, courage, personal appearance, and advancing to new frontiers.

This or something better than this comes to me in an easy and pleasurable way, for the good of all concerned. Thank you, Universe!

New Moon in Aries

Your Personal Moon Experience

Fill in the Cosmic Check-In page. Then look up the degree of the Moon on the chart below. Take note of the "I" statement on the outside of the wheel where the Moon is located. Now, locate the same degree on your own chart and make a note of the house and corresponding "I" statement. Go back to the Cosmic Check-In page and circle the two statements from the charts and read what you wrote. This will give you an idea about what to expect from this moon phase on a personal level. For more information on personalizing your *Moon Book*, go to www.BlueMoonAcademy.com and look for *How to Use the Moon Book*.

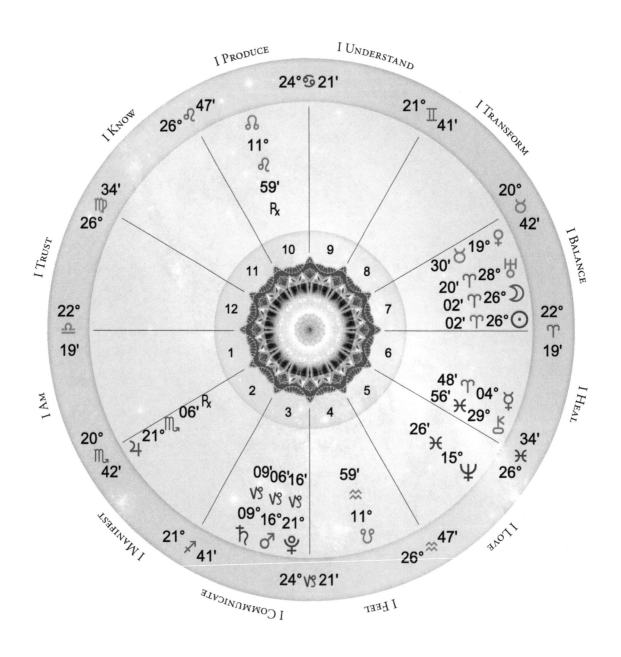

♈	Aries	♋	Cancer	♏	Scorpio	♓	Pisces	♀	Venus	♅	Uranus	☊	North Node
♉	Taurus	♌	Leo	♐	Sagittarius	☉	Sun	♂	Mars	♆	Neptune	☋	South Node
♊	Gemini	♍	Virgo	♑	Capricorn	☽	Moon	♃	Jupiter	♇	Pluto	℞	Retrograde
♎	Libra	♒	Aquarius	☿	Mercury	♄	Saturn	⚷	Chiron				

Cosmic Check-in

Aries New Moon
April 15th
6:57 PM

Take a moment to write a brief phrase for each "I" statement.
This activates all areas of your life for this creative cycle.

♈ I Am

♉ I Manifest

♊ I Communicate

♋ I Feel

♌ I Love

♍ I Heal

♎ I Balance

♏ I Transform

♐ I Understand

♑ I Produce

♒ I Know

♓ I Trust

Full Moon in Scorpio

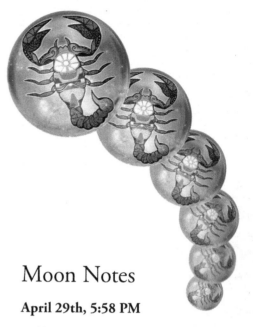

When the Sun is Opposite the Moon

Full moons are always in opposition to the Sun. This creates a feeling of tension between where you want to shine and how your feelings are flowing on a sensory level about the Sun's directive. The two forces seem like they are working against each other, yet they are on the same team displaying different techniques to obtain the same mission. The Scorpio/Taurus polarity creates tension between sharing resources and living abundantly for yourself.

Scorpio Goddess

The concept of web thinking, in which all is intrinsically interconnected and related to the whole, comes to us through the creator myths of the Pueblo and Hopi people, as Grandmother Spider. She spun a sparkling dew-dropped web and threw it up into the night sky to create the stars.

Her interdependent web of light reminds us to promote the power of community and band together to take action when important issues affect the whole. Grandmother Spider can help you appreciate your own and others' unique contributions and talents, and show you how to combine them to create a strong and sustainable web of action.

Build Your Altar

Colors Indigo, deep purple, scarlet

Numerology 6 – Fill your day with love

Tarot Card Death – The ability to make changes

Gemstones Topaz, tanzanite, onyx, obsidian

Plant remedy Manzanita – Prepares the body for transformation

Fragrance Sandalwood – Awakens your sensuality

Moon Notes

April 29th, 5:58 PM

Full Moon 9° Scorpio 39'
Full Moons are about releasing, letting go, becoming free, and recalibrating.

Statement I Transform

Body Sex organs

Mind Intensity

Spirit Transformation

Element
Water – Taking the path of least resistance, going with the flow, and creativity at it's best. Secretive, glamourous, sensual, psychic, magnetic, actress, escape artist, and healer.

Choice Points
Light Enjoyable bonding
Shadow Revealed secrets
Wisdom Scattered energies, yours or another's, cause a need for rest.

Sabian Symbol
A fellowship supper reunites old comrades.

Potential
The rewards of cherished days come forward.

1st House Moon I Am/I Transform

Umbrella Energy
Your outer appearance, the way you present yourself, the way you dress, the way you enter a room, and what you leave behind when you leave the room.

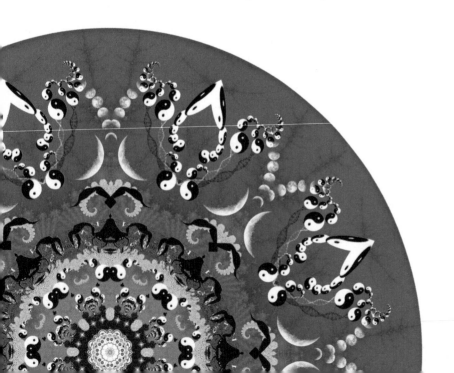

Clearing the Slate

Sixty hours before the full moon negative traits connected to the astro-sign might become activated to trigger what needs to be released during the full moon phase. You may notice a deep desire to be secretive, resist sharing money, a feeling of revenge, or the need to create control dramas. Make a list, look in the mirror, and for each negative trait, tell yourself *I am sorry, I forgive you, thank you for your awareness,* and *I love you.*

Scorpio Victories & Challenges

Say all of the statements in this section out loud. Then, underline the phrase that means the most to you. Use the phrase as your affirmation for recalibrating throughout this moon phase.

I will not compromise myself today. I know that transformation occurs when I stand tall in my truth, even if everything around me needs to die. I see death as a new beginning and know that in death comes new aliveness. I am willing to embrace transformation and open to the idea that change is in my favor. I know that in letting go, I give new life to myself. I am willing to accept that life is everchanging and in a constant state of renewal; one cannot occur without the other.

Releasing is easy when I offer myself something new. When I allow for the motion of change to stay alive, I let go with one hand and receive with the other hand. The ever-present flow and motion keeps me alive and connected to the revitalizing power of Nature. When the power of Nature becomes apparent to me, I become aware that Nature abhors a vacuum. Rejuvenation is mine when I embrace change.

Scorpio Homework

The Scorpio moon creates the urge within us to make life happen. Pay attention to these urges so you can prepare yourself for greater action, intention, and purpose.

Gratitude List

Keep this list active throughout the moon cycle. This will bring you to a level of completion so that a new cycle of opportunity can occur in your life. Be prepared for miracles!

Sky Power Yoga

Reclined Goddess on a Chair

You need one chair for the prop.

Sit on the floor close to your chair with the right side of your upper torso facing the chair seat and your lower torso close to the chair legs.

Lean back onto your left elbow and lift your right leg onto the chair seat. With your back flat on the floor, lift your left leg to rest on the chair seat next to the right leg.

Place the bottoms of your feet together in the center of the chair seat. Allow

your knees to fall towards the edges of the chair seat. Adjust your knees to allow your thighs to open comfortably.

Relax. Close your eyes. Breathe in and out slowly and deeply several times through your nose with your awareness on your reproductive organs.

Inhale deeply as you say or think to yourself the mantra *I Transform*.

Exhale slowly and relax into the pose more deeply with each out breath. Repeat as desired.

Freedom List

Say this statement out loud three times before writing your list:

I am a free spiritual being and it is my desire to be free to think and to express myself fully.

Scorpio Freedom Ideas

Now is the time to activate a game change in my life, and give up resentment, jealousy, revenge, vendettas, betrayals, blocks to transformation, destructive relationships, unhealthy joint financial situations, obstacles to having a healthy sex life, resistance to changing paradigms, and karma relating to all issues of power.

I am now free and ready to make choices beyond survival!

Full Moon in Scorpio

Your Personal Moon Experience

Fill in the Cosmic Check-In page. Then look up the degree of the Moon on the chart below. Take note of the "I" statement on the outside of the wheel where the Moon is located. Now, locate the same degree on your own chart and make

a note of the house and corresponding "I" statement. Go back to the Cosmic Check-In page, circle the two statements from the charts, and read what you wrote. This will give you an idea about what to expect from this moon phase on a personal level. For a personalized *My Moon Experience* Astrology reading with Beatrex, go to www.beatrex.com.

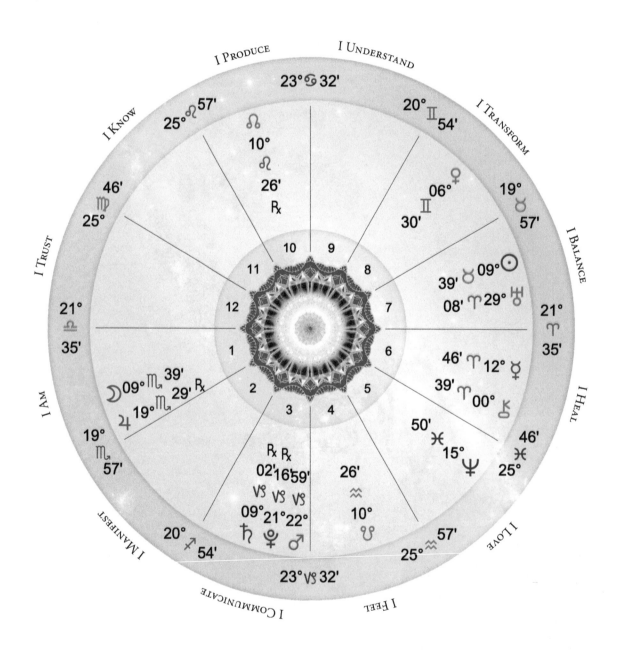

♈	Aries	♋	Cancer	♏	Scorpio	♓	Pisces	♀	Venus	♅	Uranus	☊	North Node
♉	Taurus	♌	Leo	♐	Sagittarius	☉	Sun	♂	Mars	♆	Neptune	☋	South Node
♊	Gemini	♍	Virgo	♑	Capricorn	☽	Moon	♃	Jupiter	♇	Pluto	℞	Retrograde
		♎	Libra	♒	Aquarius	☿	Mercury	♄	Saturn	⚷	Chiron		

Cosmic Check-in

Scorpio Full Moon
April 29th
5:58 PM

Take a moment to write a brief phrase for each "I" statement.
This activates all areas of your life for this creative cycle.

♏ I Transform

♐ I Understand

♑ I Produce

♒ I Know

♓ I Trust

♈ I Am

♉ I Manifest

♊ I Communicate

♋ I Feel

♌ I Love

♍ I Heal

♎ I Balance

May

May 3-4: Super Sensitivity

Remember, the intense energy is universal not personal. If you sense the fragility in the air, don't get curious and check it out. It is time to avoid negative thinking and depressing thoughts especially since they probably don't belong to you.

May 13: Mercury enters Taurus

This is a good time to work on marketing, you will know the right words to describe what you are up to and good business will come your way. Communication is commensurate to your success, keep broadcasting what you know.

May 15: Uranus enters Taurus

This is a huge game changer—the planet who governs our future is switching signs for the first time since 2011. While in Aries, Uranus motivated the actualization of personal power, as we have seen in our multitude of social and political protesting where the individual needs recognition, setting up a generation of people who will keep that theme alive. Now the revolution or need for a different future will move us into the realm of business and finance. We will become aware of new and innovative trends. How resistant we are to these changes will determine the extent of the revolution. In any event, there will be a breakdown or breakthrough in the system of business and the economic elements of power. Be prepared to give flexibility a chance.

May 15: Mars enters Aquarius

The planet of action and change moves into the land of the future. Expect to be impressed by technological advances that show us a new future. Now is the time to be updated! Get informed and be a part of this forward motion—don't get left behind.

May 15: Uranus and Mercury conjunct in Taurus

Trends are forming to put us in the know. The next seven years set a new tone for living. Be willing to ride the waves.

May 16-20: Low Vitality

Earth changes are possible. Stay safe! When endings appear, let them happen.

May 19: Venus enters Cancer

Expect a sudden urge to redecorate or remodel your home. Perhaps its time for a beauty update in your family. Have fun with this and let refinement heal you and yours.

May 20: Sun enters Gemini

Let the Sun shine brightly on you and your lifestyle. Questions to ask yourself: "How am I representing my true self?" "Is what I say and what I mean in alignment?" Duality can get you in trouble during the Gemini time. Test yourself to see how you represent both sides of any situation without the sting of judgment.

May 29: Mercury enters Gemini

Yay! Mercury is at home for now; take advantage of this and get your message out there. The marketplace is your playground, use it.

May 29: South Node coupled with Mars in Aquarius

Time for spring cleaning! Update your 'Toolbox' and throw out what is no longer relevant.

May 30-31: Super Sensitivity

The collective is at work trying to influence you. Before taking on anything at this time, make sure it is yours and not an influencing cloud of illusion.

Sunday	Monday	Tuesday	Wednesday	Thursday	Friday	Saturday
		1 ♄♃♇℞ ☽→♐ 8:19 AM 8. Enjoy manifesting self-reliance.	**2** ♄♃♇℞ 9. Pray with pure intention.	**3** ♄♃♇℞▲ ☽-V/C 5:49 PM ☽→♑ 7:06 PM 10. Find joy in the now.	**4** ♄♃♇℞▲ 11. Receive the spiritual gift.	**5** ♄♃♇℞ 3. Believe your experience.
6 ♄♃♇℞ ☽-V/C 6:48 AM ☽→♒ 7:48 AM 4. Stay connected.	**7** ♄♃♇℞ 5. Free yourself from repeating patterns.	**8** ♄♃♇℞ ☽-V/C 7:28 PM ☽→♓ 8:10 PM 6. Enjoy good health by walking outdoors.	**9** ♄♃♇℞ 7. Study with a friend.	**10** ♄♃♇℞ 8. Lead by being progressive.	**11** ♄♃♇℞ ☽-V/C 2:02 AM ☽→♈ 5:40 AM 9. Stay spiritually connected.	**12** ♄♃♇℞ 10. Recalibrate memories and move on.
13 ♄♃♇℞ Mother's Day ☽-V/C 11:04 AM ☽→♉ 11:15 AM ☿→♉ 5:41 AM 2. Have a balanced point of view.	**14** ♄♃♇℞ 3. Live in the moment.	**15** ♄♃♇℞ ● 24°♉36' - 4:47 AM ☽-V/C 1:29 PM ☽→♊ 1:43 PM ♅→♉ 8:24 AM ♂→♒ 9:56 PM 4. Keep things in order.	**16** ♄♃♇℞▼ 5. Is a trip in the air?	**17** ♄♃♇℞▼ ☽-V/C 11:17 AM ☽→♋ 2:47 PM 6. Visit an art museum.	**18** ♄♃♇℞▼ 7. Check a definition.	**19** ♄♃♇℞▼ ☽-V/C 2:14 PM ☽→♌ 4:10 PM ♀→♋ 6:12 AM 8. Be a strong leader.
20 ♄♃♇℞▼ ☽-V/C 8:29 PM ☉→♊ 7:16 PM 9. Serve with a loving heart.	**21** ♄♃♇℞ ☽→♍ 7:02 PM 10. Renew your purpose and vision.	**22** ♄♃♇℞ 2. Gather the facts, then decide.	**23** ♄♃♇℞ ☽-V/C 7:55 AM ☽→♎ 11:51 PM 3. Play with gusto.	**24** ♄♃♇℞ 4. Respect everyone on your team.	**25** ♄♃♇℞ ☽-V/C 2:03 PM 5. Versatility is necessary today.	**26** ♄♃♇℞ ☽→♏ 6:39 AM 6. Harmony in the home adds love.
27 ♄♃♇℞ 8. Using courage can fulfill a dream.	**28** ♄♃♇℞ Memorial Day ☽-V/C 10:25 AM ☽→♐ 3:28 PM 9. A pay-it-forward day.	**29** ♄♃♇℞ ○ 08°♐10' - 7:19 AM ☽-V/C 11:25 PM ☿→♊ 4:50 PM 10. Allow destiny to unfold.	**30** ♄♃♇℞▲ 2. Do a balancing yoga pose to ground.	**31** ♄♃♇℞▲ ☽→♑ 2:26 AM 3. Go enjoy being in nature.		

♈ Aries	♍ Virgo	♓ Pisces	♃ Jupiter	→ Enters	2. Balance	8. Money
♉ Taurus	♎ Libra	☉ Sun	♄ Saturn	℞ Retrograde	3. Fun	9. Spirituality
♊ Gemini	♏ Scorpio	☽ Moon	♅ Uranus	S/D Stationary Direct	4. Structure	10. Visionary
♋ Cancer	♐ Sagittarius	☿ Mercury	♆ Neptune	V/C Void-of-Course	5. Action	11. Completion
♌ Leo	♑ Capricorn	♀ Venus	♇ Pluto	▲ Super Sensitivity	6. Love	
	♒ Aquarius	♂ Mars	⚷ Chiron	▼ Low Vitality	7. Learning	

New Moon in Taurus

When the Sun is in Taurus

Taurus is the time when we see the true manifesting power, as the plants move to a higher aspiration of life and bloom. Once again, we become connected to the essence of beauty as a symbol of our divinity. Taurus is the connection between humanity and divinity. Taurus' job is to infuse matter with light through accumulating layers of substance. This is why they are such good shoppers and collectors. The more they accumulate, the more divinity they experience. This process brings about a sense of self-value which is directly commensurate to the amount of money they manifest. Personal resources are part of the pattern. Discover your value at this time.

Taurus Goddess

Today, Lakshmi, the Hindu Goddess of Abundance, walks into your life bearing gifts. She joyously showers you with success, wealth, well-being, luck, happiness, and fulfillment. Her blessings also include forgiveness and the generosity of spirit that allows you to reap the recognition for good work well done.

Working with feng shui, place a statue of Lakshmi in the left-hand corner of your room (looking in from the entrance) to honor her and to signal your receptivity. Are your hands and heart open and ready to receive? Make space for the new. Step confidently into the flow of abundance! Take Lakshmi's lead and shower everyone you meet with kindness and generosity!

Build Your Altar

Colors	Green, pink, deep red, earth tones
Numerology	4 – Keep things in order
Tarot Card	Hierophant – The ability to listen, inner-knowing
Gemstones	Topaz, agate, smoky quartz, jade, rose quartz
Plant Remedy	Angelica – Connecting Heaven and Earth
Fragrance	Rose – Opening the heart

Moon Notes

May 15th, 4:47 AM

New Moon 24° Taurus 36'
New Moons are about manifestation, planting seeds, and becoming fruitful.

Statement	I Manifest
Body	Neck
Mind	Collector
Spirit	Accumulation

Element
Earth – Practical, determined, structured, enduring, stubborn, traditional, stable, and stuck inside the box.

Choice Points
Light	Collective well-being
Shadow	Loss of identity
Wisdom	An ascended Master is trying to get your attention.

Sabian Symbol
A vast public park.

Potential
Maintenance is required to accept your stewardship.

1st House Moon I Am/I Manifest

Umbrella Energy
Your outer appearance, the way you present yourself, the way you dress, the way you enter a room, and what you leave behind when you leave the room.

Karmic Awakening
Aries/Libra – The "I" versus "We"

Taurus Victories & Challenges

Say all of the statements in this section out loud. Then, underline the phrase that means the most to you. Use the phrase as your affirmation for recalibrating throughout this moon phase.

Everything is possible for me today. My possibilities are endless. I have the power within me to make all of my dreams come true. I have the tools to make my talent a reality. I have the power to identify with my talent. Today, I focus my attention and intention on manifesting with my talent and, in so doing, I transform my ideas into reality. I recognize the part of me that is connected to the cosmic source of ideas and I express that source within me to manifest my creative power. I see my possibilities and act on them today. I am the creative power. I am all-knowing. I am an individual. There is no one else like me. I can manifest anything I desire. I intend it, I allow it, so be it.

Rules for Manifesting

Know what you want. Write it down. Say it out loud. Recognize that because you thought it, it can be so. Release your limiting beliefs. Override your limiting beliefs with power statements. Act as if you have already manifested your idea. Lastly, value yourself!

Taurus Homework

Taureans manifest best when buying, selling, and owning real estate, gardening and landscaping, selling and collecting art, manufacturing and selling fine furniture, singing or acting, and as a restaurateur, antique dealer, or interior designer.

The Taurus moon asks us to infuse light into form and, in so doing, the bridge between humanity and divinity is actualized and we can assume our stewardship in the physical world. When we release Spirit into matter, we become open to the idea that accumulation and actualization set us free to experience the abundance available to us here on Earth. Go shopping!

Victory List

Acknowledge what you have overcome.
Keep this list active during this moon cycle.
Honoring victory allows you to accept success.

Sky Power Yoga

Seated Neck Rolls

You need one chair for the prop.

Sit one hand-width forward from the back of the chair. Back is straight and feet are placed hip-width apart on the floor. If your feet require more solid contact with the floor, place pillows or folded towels under your feet.

Relax and close your eyes. Breathe in and out slowly and deeply several times through your nose, with your awareness on your throat.

As you exhale, drop your head forward rolling the right ear toward the right shoulder.

Inhale and tip your chin up slightly while you envision the energy of your breath coming into

your neck. Say or think to yourself the mantra *I Manifest*.

Exhale softly and slowly as you roll your head forward and to the opposite direction with the left ear towards the left shoulder.

Inhale, tipping your chin slightly up and repeating the mantra, then exhale rolling back toward the right shoulder. Repeat as desired.

Manifesting List

Taurus Manifesting Ideas

Now is the time to focus on manifesting success, money, property, luxury, beauty, personal value, and pleasure.

This or something better than this comes to me in an easy and pleasurable way, for the good of all concerned. Thank you, Universe!

New Moon in Taurus

Your Personal Moon Experience

Fill in the Cosmic Check-In page. Then look up the degree of the Moon on the chart below. Take note of the "I" statement on the outside of the wheel where the Moon is located. Now, locate the same degree on your own chart and make a note of the house and corresponding "I" statement. Go back to the Cosmic Check-In page and circle the two statements from the charts and read what you wrote. This will give you an idea about what to expect from this moon phase on a personal level. For more information on personalizing your *Moon Book*, go to www.BlueMoonAcademy.com and look for *How to Use the Moon Book*.

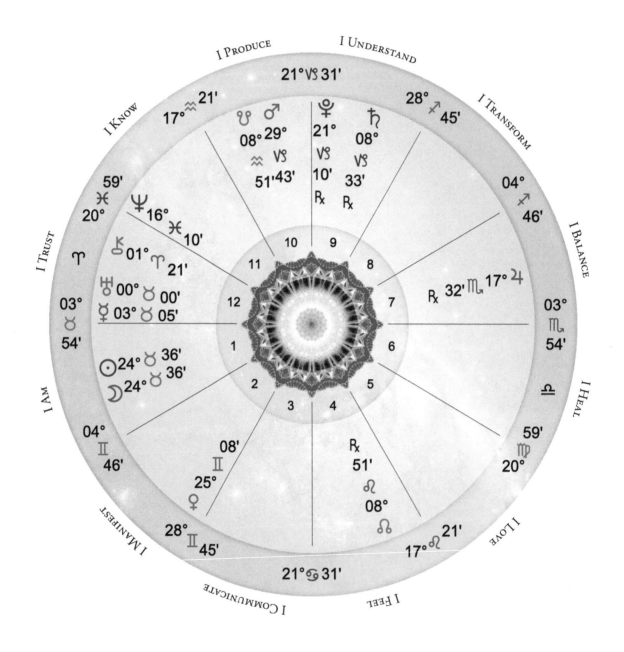

♈	Aries	♋	Cancer	♏	Scorpio	♓	Pisces	♀	Venus	♅	Uranus	☊	North Node
♉	Taurus	♌	Leo	♐	Sagittarius	☉	Sun	♂	Mars	♆	Neptune	☋	South Node
♊	Gemini	♍	Virgo	♑	Capricorn	☿	Mercury	♃	Jupiter	♇	Pluto	℞	Retrograde
		♎	Libra	♒	Aquarius	☽	Moon	♄	Saturn	⚷	Chiron		

Cosmic Check-in

Taurus New Moon
May 15th
4:47 AM

Take a moment to write a brief phrase for each "I" statement.
This activates all areas of your life for this creative cycle.

♉ I Manifest

♊ I Communicate

♋ I Feel

♌ I Love

♍ I Heal

♎ I Balance

♏ I Transform

♐ I Understand

♑ I Produce

♒ I Know

♓ I Trust

♈ I Am

Full Moon in Sagittarius

When the Sun is Opposite the Moon

Full moons are always in opposition to the Sun. This creates a feeling of tension between where you want to shine and how your feelings are flowing on a sensory level about the Sun's directive. The two forces seem like they are working against each other, yet they are on the same team displaying different techniques to obtain the same mission. The Sagittarius/Gemini polarity creates tension between the quest for higher knowledge and the need for academic accolades.

Sagittarius Goddess

Pythia was the title bestowed upon the priestess who channeled the Oracle of Delphi at the Temple of Apollo. The rambling prophecies she spoke were induced by breathing the vapors rising out of the chasm in the rocks, at a site formerly dedicated to the great Earth Goddess, Gaia.

Allow yourself quiet meditation time with your favorite divination tool (Tarot cards, pendulum, automatic writing) and give yourself over to messages you receive. Remember that Pythia calls forth her art through the magic of breathwork, which operates without hallucinogenic vapors! Seek the messages she delivers from the wisdom and stored history of the Earth. Find a rock to sit on and breathe!

Build Your Altar

Colors	Deep purple, turquoise, royal blue
Numerology	10 - Allow destiny to unfold
Tarot Card	Temperance – Balancing the present with the past, updating yourself
Gemstone	Turquoise
Plant remedy	Madia – Seeing and hitting the target
Fragrance	Magnolia – Expanded beauty

Moon Notes

May 29th, 7:19 AM

Full Moon 8° Sagittarius 10'
Full Moons are about releasing, letting go, becoming free, and recalibrating.

Statement	I Understand
Body	Thighs
Mind	Philosophical
Spirit	Inspiration

Element
Fire – Igniting, dissolving, accelerating, cleansing, advancing awareness, impatience, leadership, passion, and vitality.

Choice Points
Light	Step-by-step guidance
Shadow	Hasty reactions
Wisdom	Offered a choice, resistance wanes and judgements are transformed.

Sabian Symbol
A mother leads her small child step by step up a steep stairway.

Potential
Trusting the process of development.

6th House Moon I Heal/I Understand

Umbrella Energy
The way you manage your body and its appearance.

Karmic Awakening
Sagittarius/Gemini – The difference between a cosmic mind and an academic mind.

Clearing the Slate

Sixty hours before the full moon negative traits connected to the astro-sign might become activated to trigger what needs to be released during the full moon phase. You may notice a sudden urge to be excessive, to resist reality by exaggerating, to speak before thinking, to be blunt, or to use unfiltered language. Make a list, look in the mirror, and for each negative trait, tell yourself *I am sorry, I forgive you, thank you for your awareness,* and *I love you.*

Sagittarius Victories & Challenges

Say all of the statements in this section out loud. Then, underline the phrase that means the most to you. Use the phrase as your affirmation for recalibrating throughout this moon phase.

Today, I blend my old self with my new self, my physical reality with my spiritual awareness, my positive thoughts with my negative thoughts, my past with my present, my feminine with my masculine, my rewards with my losses, my ups with my downs, and my higher self with my lower self. It is a day for me to refine and fine tune my life by looking at my extremes. I recognize what inspires me and what keeps me stuck. I find my center today by acknowledging my extremes. I am aware that balance comes to those who are able to locate the space in the center of these opposite energy fields. When I am in my center, my polarities are in motion. Healing cannot occur unless my polarities are moving and I know that healing is motion.

I am ready for a healing today and know that by visiting my opposites and determining their vast opposition to each other, I can find the paradoxes that I have chosen for myself and begin to heal. I am willing to experiment with this blending of opposites and become the alchemist of my own life. When I blend all aspects of myself, rather than separating them, I can truly become whole. Today is a day to integrate, rather than separate, in order to release the spark of light that stays prisoner when my polarities are in operation. When I find balance, motion occurs and the Law of Harmony takes over, putting paradoxical energies to rest, thus breaking the crystallization of polarity. The Law of Harmony is beauty in motion, promoting the flow of color, light, sound, and movement into form. Balance is a condition that keeps my spark in motion. I become the vertical line in the center of polarity today and carry the secret of balance. Balance cannot be my goal, motion is my goal today. When I am in motion, I can take action to evolve and to express all of myself freely.

Sagittarius Homework

Now is the time to use your physical body to release the feeling of being caged in by people or circumstances. Choose an activity that burns away confinement and allows you to feel the power of your passion.

The Sagittarius moon awakens us to know the spark of light that lives in our heart, thus elevating love in ourselves and in our world. This is when we come to realize what is in our highest and best good and we can begin to recalibrate all that is not lovable in our lives.

Gratitude List

Keep this list active throughout the moon cycle. This will bring you to a level of completion so that a new cycle of opportunity can occur in your life. Be prepared for miracles!

Sky Power Yoga

Seated Pure Hip

You need one chair for the prop.

Sit one hand-width forward from the back of the chair. Back is straight and feet are placed hip-width apart on the floor. If your feet require more solid contact with the floor, place pillows or folded towels under your feet.

Bring your right foot up over your left knee. Rest your right ankle on your lower-left thigh.

Relax. Close your eyes. Breathe in and out slowly and deeply several times through your nose with your awareness on your thigh.

Inhale deeply and lengthen your back. Say or think to yourself the mantra *I Understand.*

Exhale slowly as you hinge at the hips and shift your weight gently forward.

Remain for several breaths. Inhale, engage your abdominals, and return your upper torso to an upright position. Repeat as desired.

Freedom List

Say this statement out loud three times before writing your list:

I am a free spiritual being and it is my desire to be free to think and to express myself fully.

Sagittarius
Recalibrating Ideas

Now is the time to activate a game change in my life, and give up belief systems that no longer apply, attitudes that are not uplifting to me, addiction to excess and risk, the need to exaggerate based on low self-esteem, dishonesty, being too blunt, staying in the future and avoiding the NOW, overriding fear by being too optimistic, and preaching.

I am now free and ready to make choices beyond survival!

109

Full Moon in Sagittarius

Your Personal Moon Experience

Fill in the Cosmic Check-In page. Then look up the degree of the Moon on the chart below. Take note of the "I" statement on the outside of the wheel where the Moon is located. Now, locate the same degree on your own chart and make

a note of the house and corresponding "I" statement. Go back to the Cosmic Check-In page, circle the two statements from the charts, and read what you wrote. This will give you an idea about what to expect from this moon phase on a personal level. For a personalized *My Moon Experience* Astrology reading with Beatrex, go to www.beatrex.com.

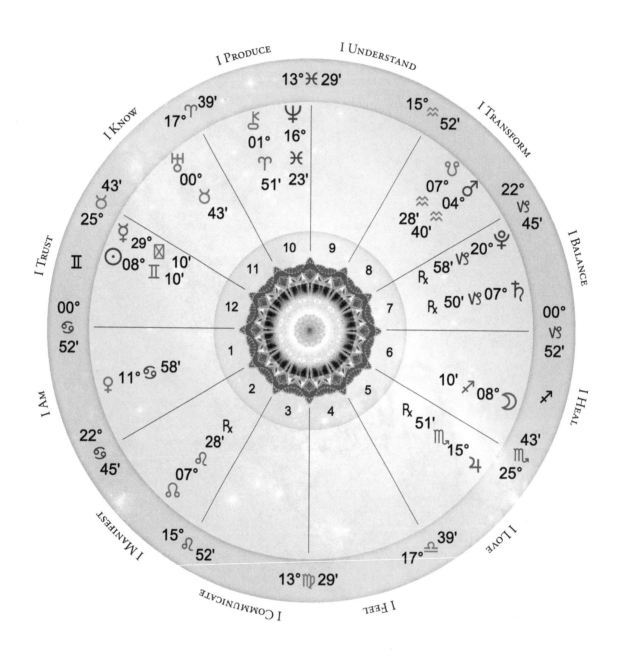

♈ Aries	♋ Cancer	♏ Scorpio	♓ Pisces	♀ Venus	♅ Uranus	☊ North Node
♉ Taurus	♌ Leo	♐ Sagittarius	☉ Sun	♂ Mars	♆ Neptune	☋ South Node
♊ Gemini	♍ Virgo	♑ Capricorn	☽ Moon	♃ Jupiter	♇ Pluto	℞ Retrograde
	♎ Libra	♒ Aquarius	☿ Mercury	♄ Saturn	⚷ Chiron	

Cosmic Check-in

Sagittarius Full Moon
May 29th
7:19 AM

Take a moment to write a brief phrase for each "I" statement.
This activates all areas of your life for this creative cycle.

♐ I Understand

♑ I Produce

♒ I Know

♓ I Trust

♈ I Am

♉ I Manifest

♊ I Communicate

♋ I Feel

♌ I Love

♍ I Heal

♎ I Balance

♏ I Transform

June

June 10-14: Low Vitality

Expect to feel a bit grumpy due to an undertow on the energy zone. Spend the day at the spa so you can get uplifted. A good day in bed binge watching your favorite TV series is a really good idea as well. Earth has a very faint heartbeat right now. This could create earth changes. Stay close to home and get rest.

June 12: Mercury enters Cancer

The pebble hits the pond awakening all sorts of feelings. Now is the time to let the feelings speak out loud and release them into the atmosphere, never to be an issue again.

June 13: Venus enters Leo

This urge to dance and have a party gets off to a slow start due to Low Vitality. Make your plans for after the 14th and any celebration that is in the air will work better.

June 13: South Node and Mars dancing in Aquarius

We move into the realm of service to each other making the world a better place. Expect a push to place you on the streets ready to help the homeless. Or, to the other extreme, moving into a place of total decadence where your movement is valued as a major game changer.

June 18: Neptune retrograde in Pisces until November 24

This is a time when the idea of escaping into fantasy becomes a survival technique. What is your mode of escape? Is it work, food, projects, cocktail time, drugs, or excessive sex or sleep? The pain of reality puts this fantasy into operation. Begin by facing the reality button and allowing yourself the consciousness of knowing.

June 21: Sun enters Cancer – Summer Solstice

Time to see what you have manifested from the Spring Equinox and where you go from here in order to harvest what is needed for winter. Ask the Guardians to keep you going for the next three months.

June 26: Mars retrograde in Aquarius until August 27

This is a time when the raw energy of Mars is unavailable and a creeping exhaustion occurs. Don't let your ego-mind tell you that you are bad or wrong for being tired. This is a challenge to learn to live with what *is*.

June 27-28: Super Sensitivity

The chaos will push you to go faster, but it's an illusion. Slow down and you will be fine. Notice if you are thinking negatively, if so, stop, or it will bring on a depression like you have never had before.

June 27: Moon and Saturn conjunct in Capricorn

Watch out for feelings being squelched. Remember the Moon is all about feelings and Saturn is all about thinking. Your thoughts block your feelings and/or your feelings drown your thinking.

June 27: North Node conjunct Mercury in Leo

This could lead you to a new invention. Something that bends light and time in a way that advances the idea of a time machine.

June 27: South Node dancing with retrograde Mars in Aquarius

Time to slow down and see what you keep holding onto that is no longer needed in this time frame. Whatever it is, you must face the fact that it is not necessary anymore. It is stealing energy from you and making you feel exhausted.

June 28: Mercury enters Leo

This is a good time to focus your mind on being loving rather than analytical. Write love letters and replace negative thinking with loving thoughts.

Sunday	Monday	Tuesday	Wednesday	Thursday	Friday	Saturday
					1 ♄♃♇℞ ☽-V/C 8:36 PM 4. Your stability supports others.	2 ♄♃♇℞ ☽→♒ 3:06 PM 5. Variety enlivens everyone's day.
3 ♄♃♇℞ ☽-V/C 10:09 PM 6. Make your home a safe haven.	4 ♄♃♇℞ 7. Analyze the details to get the big picture.	5 ♄♃♇℞ ☽→♓ 3:53 AM 8. Share your victories with friends.	6 ♄♃♇℞ ☽-V/C 11:34 PM 9. Your heart sees the humanity in everyone.	7 ♄♃♇℞ ☽→♈ 2:25 PM 10. Get ahead, upgrade technology.	8 ♄♃♇℞ 11. Trust the Universe to support you.	9 ♄♃♇℞ ☽-V/C 12:36 PM ☽→♉ 9:03 PM 3. Be a friend and give someone a call.
10 ♄♃♇℞▼ 4. Your organizational skills are needed.	11 ♄♃♇℞▼ ☽-V/C 8:28 PM ☽→♊ 11:52 PM 5. Make changes now and freedom is yours.	12 ♄♃♇℞▼ ☿→♋-1:01 PM 6. It's beneficial to listen to your body.	13 ♄♃♇℞▼ ● 22°♊44' - 12:43 PM ☽-V/C 12:43 PM ♀→♌-2:55 PM 7. The quiet voice within speaks truth.	14 ♄♃♇℞▼ ☽→♋ 12:19 AM 8. There is enough for all to succeed.	15 ♄♃♇℞ ☽-V/C 9:18 AM 9. Pray sincerely for all to know love.	16 ♄♃♇℞ ☽→♌ 12:20 AM 10. Is there a goal that needs a vision?
17 ♄♃♇℞ Father's Day ☽-V/C 8:25 PM 2. Be gentle with people.	18 ♄♃♇♆℞ ☽→♍ 1:40 AM ♆SR-16°♓29' 4:28 PM 3. Play joyfully, you will feel better.	19 ♄♃♇♆℞ 4. Work with the players in your group.	20 ♄♃♇♆℞ ☽-V/C 3:50 AM ☽→♎ 5:29 AM 5. Be conscious of how you drive.	21 ♄♃♇♆℞ ☽V/C 6:33 PM ☉→♋ 3:08 AM Summer Solstice 6. Spruce up the house for a party.	22 ♄♃♇♆℞ ☽→♏ 12:10 PM 7. Study a topic that intrigues you.	23 ♄♃♇♆℞ 8. Respect your leadership abilities.
24 ♄♃♇♆℞ ☽-V/C 6:59 AM ☽→♐ 9:29 PM 9. To grow spiritually is Divine Grace.	25 ♄♃♇♆℞ 10. Have a pioneering attitude.	26 ♂♄♃♇♆℞ ☽-V/C 5:53 AM ♂SR-9°♒13' - 2:06 PM 2. Take the first intuitive hit you get.	27 ♂♄♃♇♆℞▲ ☽→♑ 8:52 AM ○ 6°♑28' - 9:52 PM 3. Choose to be happy.	28 ♂♄♃♇♆℞▲ ☿→♌ 10:17 PM 4. Dependability is a virtue.	29 ♂♄♃♇♆℞ ☽-V/C 1:57 AM ☽→♒ 9:36 PM 5. Versitility leads to understanding.	30 ♂♄♃♇♆℞ 6. Heal by singing along with the radio.

♈ Aries	♍ Virgo	♓ Pisces	♃ Jupiter	→ Enters	2. Balance	8. Money
♉ Taurus	♎ Libra	☉ Sun	♄ Saturn	℞ Retrograde	3. Fun	9. Spirituality
♊ Gemini	♏ Scorpio	☽ Moon	♅ Uranus	S/D Stationary Direct	4. Structure	10. Visionary
♋ Cancer	♐ Sagittarius	☿ Mercury	♆ Neptune	V/C Void-of-Course	5. Action	11. Completion
♌ Leo	♑ Capricorn	♀ Venus	♇ Pluto	▲ Super Sensitivity	6. Love	
	♒ Aquarius	♂ Mars	⚷ Chiron	▼ Low Vitality	7. Learning	

New Moon in Gemini

When the Sun is in Gemini

This is a time when the ability to communicate is at the top of the priority list. Allow your thoughts to lead you to a formula for success so you can put your thoughts into action. Then, find the appropriate soapbox to stand on so your message can be heard. Right now is the time to make your message clear, enlightening, witty, and thought-provoking. Your bright mind is at its high throne and waiting for an audience. Try blogging, do a show on YouTube, join Toastmasters, write that screenplay, film yourself doing a travel show, start a discussion group, or write a newsletter for your neighborhood. Most of all, put your bright mind to work!

Gemini Goddess

Some of Zeus's favorite consorts were the nymphs who lived on Mount Kithairon. One in particular, Echo, incurred Zeus' wife Hera's wrath. As punishment for trying to protect Zeus, Hera cursed Echo with only being able to speak the last few words spoken to her. In love with Narcissus, Echo was unable to speak her own truth, and watched as Narcissus fell in love with himself, abetted by the words he spoke that Echo was forced to repeat back to him. After he died, Echo physically wasted away, leaving only the sound of her voice.

During this Gemini full moon, attend to your communications! Be curious about what ripples your speech and writing may generate. What reverberates and repeats? Is it your truth?

Build Your Altar

Colors	Bright yellow, orange, multi-colors
Numerology	7 – The quiet voice within speaks the truth
Tarot Card	Lovers – Connecting to wholeness
Gemstones	Yellow diamond, citrine
Plant Remedy	Morning Glory – Thinking with your heart not your head
Fragrance	Iris – The ability to focus the mind

Moon Notes

June 13th, 12:43 PM

New Moon 22° Gemini 44'
New Moons are about manifestation, planting seeds, and becoming fruitful.

Statement	I Communicate
Body	Lungs and hands
Mind	Intellect
Spirit	Intelligence

Element
Air – The breath of life that allows the mind to achieve new insights and fresh perspectives, inspiration, active and abstract dreaming, and freedom from attachments.

Dropping Moon
Write your intentions early, before the Moon goes void.

Choice Points

Light	Spiritual growth
Shadow	Creative unrest
Wisdom	Like a chameleon, you are able to adapt your identity to fit any situation.

Sabian Symbol
Three fledglings in a nest high in a tree.

Potential
Caution, don't leave early you are not ready to go yet.

10th House Moon
I Produce/I Communicate

Umbrella Energy
Your approach to status, career, honor, and prestige, and why you chose your Father.

Gemini Victories & Challenges

Say all of the statements in this section out loud. Then, underline the phrase that means the most to you. Use the phrase as your affirmation for recalibrating throughout this moon phase.

I am dark. I am light. I am day. I am night. The extremes in life exist within me, completing themselves in reality. The "I" that is "we" lives within me. I am one in the same. I am both.

I know that flow comes from accepting my opposite natures. Today, I accept my opposites and get into the flow. I am aware today of how my judgments separate me from people, events, experiences, and, most of all, from myself. Today, I am going to see where I have separated all of the parts of myself and begin to integrate into wholeness through acceptance and understanding. I begin by breathing. I breathe in wholeness and breathe out separation. I understand that breath is life and that life includes all facets of my experience to gain awareness. I know that I am Heaven. I know that I am Earth. I know that I am masculine. I know that I am feminine. Today, I become unified. Today, I integrate into wholeness. I breathe into all of these aspects of myself, knowing that in my totality I am connected to Oneness. The "I" that is "we" lives within me. I am one in the same. I am both.

Gemini Homework

Geminis manifest best through broadcasting and journalism, as a speech coach, comedian, political satirist, gossip columnist, negotiator, media specialist, manicurist, salesperson, teacher, or travel consultant.

Expect to awaken your will on seven levels...

- The will to direct – through the power of your original intention.

- The will to love – stimulating goodwill among humankind through cooperation.

- The will to act – by laying foundations for a happier world.

- The will to cooperate – the desire and demand for right relationships.

- The will to know – to think correctly and creatively so that every man/woman can find their outstanding characteristics.

- The will to persist – to be one with your light and represent the ideal standard for living.

- The will to organize – to carry forward direct inspiration through groups of goodwill.

Victory List

Acknowledge what you have overcome.
Keep this list active during this moon cycle.
Honoring victory allows you to accept success.

Sky Power Yoga

Seated Camel

You need one chair
for the prop.

Sit one hand-width forward
from the back of the chair.
Your back is straight and
your feet are placed hip-
width apart on the floor.

Lengthen the spine and
slightly tuck your chin.
Then interlace your fingers
behind your back with your
knuckles facing down.

Relax. Close your eyes.
Breathe in and out slowly
and deeply several times
through your nose with

your awareness on your
lungs and hands.

Inhale deeply. Lift your
chest and press your hands
down and backwards. Say
or think to yourself the
mantra *I Communicate*.

Exhale slowly. Release
the pose by bending your
elbows and dropping your
chest back to normal.
Repeat as desired.

Manifesting List

Gemini Manifesting Ideas

Now is the time to focus on manifesting communications, a promotion, technology, ideas, non-judgmental communication, thinking outside of duality, a quiet mind, charisma and charm, and flirting.

This or something better than this comes to me in an easy and pleasurable way, for the good of all concerned. Thank you, Universe!

New Moon in Gemini

Your Personal Moon Experience

Fill in the Cosmic Check-In page. Then look up the degree of the Moon on the chart below. Take note of the "I" statement on the outside of the wheel where the Moon is located. Now, locate the same degree on your own chart and make a note of the house and corresponding "I" statement. Go back to the Cosmic Check-In page and circle the two statements from the charts and read what you wrote. This will give you an idea about what to expect from this moon phase on a personal level. For more information on personalizing your *Moon Book*, go to www.BlueMoonAcademy.com and look for *How to Use the Moon Book*.

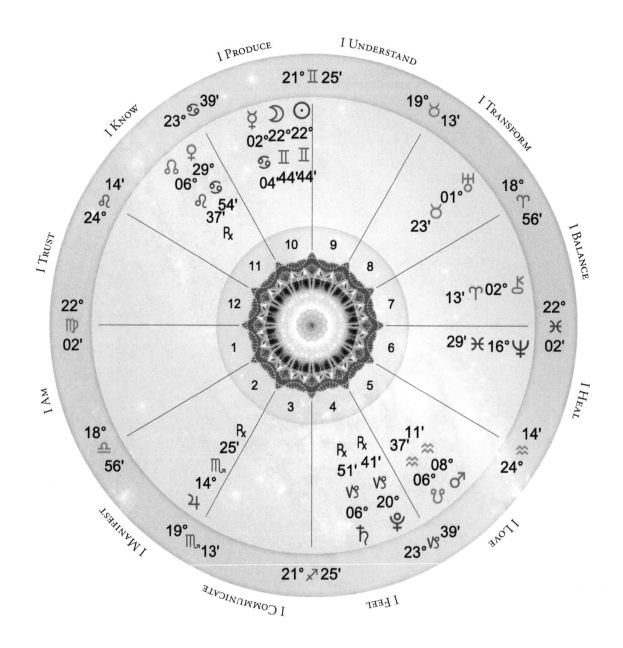

♈	Aries	♋	Cancer	♏	Scorpio	♓	Pisces	♀	Venus	♅	Uranus	☊	North Node
♉	Taurus	♌	Leo	♐	Sagittarius	☉	Sun	♂	Mars	♆	Neptune	☋	South Node
♊	Gemini	♍	Virgo	♑	Capricorn	☽	Moon	♃	Jupiter	♇	Pluto	℞	Retrograde
♎	Libra	♒	Aquarius	☿	Mercury	♄	Saturn	⚷	Chiron				

Cosmic Check-in

Gemini New Moon
June 13th
12:43 PM

Take a moment to write a brief phrase for each "I" statement.
This activates all areas of your life for this creative cycle.

♊ I Communicate

♋ I Feel

♌ I Love

♍ I Heal

♎ I Balance

♏ I Transform

♐ I Understand

♑ I Produce

♒ I Know

♓ I Trust

♈ I Am

♉ I Manifest

Full Moon in Capricorn

When the Sun is Opposite the Moon

Full moons are always in opposition to the Sun. This creates a feeling of tension between where you want to shine and how your feelings are flowing on a sensory level about the Sun's directive. The two forces seem like they are working against each other, yet they are on the same team displaying different techniques to obtain the same mission. The Capricorn/Cancer polarity creates tension between the quest for status and the need to feel secure.

Capricorn Goddess

The Goddess of hearth and home, Hestia, was once known as Chief of the Goddesses, and Hestia, the First and Last. Representing the central source, she embodies the virtues of a calm, stable, supportive, and well-centered mother and loving home-base. Hestia's symbols are the sacred flame and the circle. Choosing to stay home on Mount Olympus, she manages the estate and dependably provides a safe haven of unconditional love for all, even strangers. Connected by an umbilical cord at Delphi to the molten core of the Earth, Hestia's hearth flame will never be extinguished.

Allow your energy to tap into that root, running directly to the center of the Earth, and energize your ability to source and sustain your vision of your home, your community, and the Earth as sacred sanctuary.

Build Your Altar

Colors	Forest green, earth tones
Numerology	3 – Choose to be happy
Tarot Card	Devil – Confinement, attachment to form, look at the broader view
Gemstones	Smoky quartz, topaz, garnet
Plant remedy	Rosemary – Activates appropriate memory
Fragrance	Frankincense – Assists the Soul's entry into the body

Moon Notes

June 27th, 9:52 PM

Full Moon 6° Capricorn 28'
   Full Moons are about releasing, letting go, becoming free, and recalibrating.

Statement	I Produce
Body	Knees
Mind	Authority issues
Spirit	Self-reliance

Element
   Earth – Practical, determined, structured, enduring, stubborn, traditional, stable, and stuck inside the box.

Choice Points

Light	Authority
Shadow	Control
Wisdom	Give your logical, analytical self a rest.

Sabian Symbol
   A veiled prophet speaks, seized by the power of a god.

Potential
   It's difficult to know whether you should trust the message or not.

11th House Moon I Know/I Produce

Umbrella Energy
   Your approach to friends, social consciousness, teamwork, community service, and the future.

Clearing the Slate

Sixty hours before the full moon negative traits connected to the astro-sign might become activated to trigger what needs to be released during the full moon phase. You may notice a sudden burden of responsibility taking over your experience of life, of paying too much attention to status and position, of no time to feel compassionate, and of challenging authorities. Make a list, look in the mirror, and for each negative trait, tell yourself *I am sorry, I forgive you, thank you for your awareness,* and *I love you.*

Capricorn Victories & Challenges

Say all of the statements in this section out loud. Then, underline the phrase that means the most to you. Use the phrase as your affirmation for recalibrating throughout this moon phase.

I feel limited. I feel confined. I feel stuck. I feel there is no way out. Perhaps I am the target of someone's envy or jealousy, or perhaps I am jealous or I am envious. Maybe I am spending too much time in the outer world and putting too much value on material rewards, things, and possessions. Maybe I am trying to possess someone or limit their view or choice. I may feel there are no choices. Maybe I am living by someone else's rules and beliefs and forgot how to think for myself. I could also be overcome by fear and too terrorized to look at anything at all.

Today, I see and feel the limits of placing the source of love outside myself. I have tunnel vision and I seem to have forgotten to look at my options. I must ask myself today, "How many ways can I look at my life, my situation, or my perceived problems?" Today, I must expand my view to encompass 360-degrees instead of only 180-degrees. I begin by acknowledging to myself that today is the worst it is going to get. I know deep within me that if I allow myself to truly experience my bottom, the top will become visible to me. It is time to look at the brighter side. Begin by identifying the problem by writing it down on a piece of paper. Start with the phrase, "The problem is_____." Fill in the blank. Then, list as many solutions to the problem as you can. List at least three. Then, say these solutions out loud every day until the answer comes to you through a person, an idea, an event, or a choice.

Capricorn Homework

Put on a good pair of walking shoes and get ready to walk your blues away. It is time to get outside and feel the loving power of Mother Earth. The green of the trees refreshes your stagnant energy while you exhaust yourself to a point of vulnerability. Then, and only then, will you feel freedom. Give yourself permission to throw your watch away and learn to live in the moment.

The Capricorn moon is the reincarnation of Spirit emerging from the dark waters of our past emotions and releasing us from our fear of change and our fear of loss. Awaken your powerful and positive spiritual connection to be open to new possibilities. Ask yourself to release your emotional loyalty to the past. We are reminded of our need for material and emotional security at this time. In order to ensure this, we must learn to build a foundation for ourselves that is lit from within, made from the materials of love, goodwill, and intelligence.

Gratitude List

Keep this list active throughout the moon cycle. This will bring you to a level of completion so that a new cycle of opportunity can occur in your life. Be prepared for miracles!

Sky Power Yoga

Seated Egg Beaters

You need two bath towels and one or more pillows for the prop.

Nest two towels, fold in quarters, and place on the chair. Place the pillow on top of the towels. Sit on the chair to see if your feet hang freely without touching the floor. Add additional pillows or folded towels to elevate you so that your feet don't touch the floor.

Sit one hand-width forward from the back of the chair. Back is straight and head is neutral. Reach behind with both hands to hold the side edges of the chair.

Relax. Close your eyes. Breathe in and out slowly several times through your nose with your awareness on your knees.

Swing your feet forward, out, and around with each foot circling in the opposite direction like an egg beater. The right foot circles clockwise, the left counterclockwise. Allow the movement of the right foot to propel the left. This movement gives a relaxing

 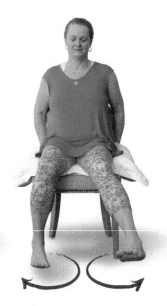

massage to the knee joint and surrounding muscles.

Inhale deeply and say or think the mantra *I Produce.*

Exhale as you slowly circle your feet. Once your breath is fully exhaled, pause, and repeat as desired.

Freedom List

Say this statement out loud three times before writing your list:

*I am a free spiritual being and it is my desire to be free to think
and to express myself fully.*

Capricorn
Recalibrating Ideas

Now is the time to activate a game change in my life, and give up obstacles to success, authority issues, sorrow and sadness, fear that blocks me, arrogance, irritability, limitations of time, priorities that are no longer valid, control and domination, the need to do it all alone, and taking on excessive responsibility.

From this day forward I resolve to be true — first to myself and my highest self, and then to the highest self in me which is the Source of Love That I Am.

127

Full Moon in Capricorn

Your Personal Moon Experience

Fill in the Cosmic Check-In page. Then look up the degree of the Moon on the chart below. Take note of the "I" statement on the outside of the wheel where the Moon is located. Now, locate the same degree on your own chart and make a note of the house and corresponding "I" statement. Go back to the Cosmic Check-In page, circle the two statements from the charts, and read what you wrote. This will give you an idea about what to expect from this moon phase on a personal level. For a personalized *My Moon Experience* Astrology reading with Beatrex, go to www.beatrex.com.

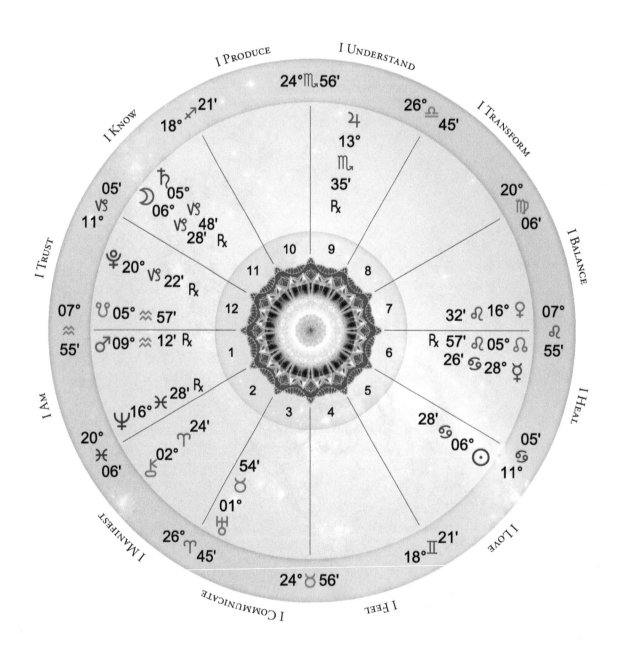

♈	Aries	♋	Cancer

♈ Aries   ♋ Cancer   ♏ Scorpio   ♓ Pisces   ♀ Venus   ♅ Uranus   ☊ North Node

♉ Taurus   ♌ Leo   ♐ Sagittarius   ☉ Sun   ♂ Mars   ♆ Neptune   ☋ South Node

♊ Gemini   ♍ Virgo   ♑ Capricorn   ☽ Moon   ☿ Mercury   ♇ Pluto   ℞ Retrograde

♎ Libra   ♒ Aquarius   ♃ Jupiter   ♄ Saturn   ⚷ Chiron

Cosmic Check-in

Capricorn Full Moon
June 27th
9:52 PM

Take a moment to write a brief phrase for each "I" statement.
This activates all areas of your life for this creative cycle.

♑ I Produce

♒ I Know

♓ I Trust

♈ I Am

♉ I Manifest

♊ I Communicate

♋ I Feel

♌ I Love

♍ I Heal

♎ I Balance

♏ I Transform

♐ I Understand

July

July 4: Chiron retrograde in Aries until 2019

Healing energy moves from water (emotions) to fire (influence), so expect a game-changing process to occur with healing. This healing will be fast and move you beyond the pain, bringing on an alchemical recalibration that actually resets your process.

July 9: Venus enters Virgo

Time to dance with health and healing.

July 10: Jupiter goes direct in Virgo

Expect attention to move from details to broad strokes. The Virgo aspect is looking for a larger application.

July 10: South Node conjunct Mars in Aquarius

Been there, done that. Expect to become unstoppable. Going with the flow is the proper course of action. Watch out for interference from cut throats who desire to win at any cost.

July 11-12: Low Vitality

Many pathways are available for action at this time. Pace yourself so burnout won't happen.

July 12: Moon and Sun in Cancer opposite Pluto in Capricorn

When secrets surface, let them come forward and ask for transformation.

July 12-17: Jupiter in Scorpio opposite Uranus in Taurus

An overwhelming need to know could take over and create a breakthrough if you can let it be. If not, explosive rebellious action will do the work.

July 22: Sun enters Leo

Time to shine knowing full well that the brightness of the Sun nurtures your essential self. Allow your true potential to be manifested.

July 24-25: Super Sensitivity

An attitude of gratitude can help you move through this time period so that negative thoughts won't permeate your field.

July 25: Mercury retrograde in Leo until August 18

Time to allow your heart-mind to speak. This is a true expression of happiness and leads to bliss. Let it be.

July 27: Moon, Mars, and South Node tripled in Aquarius

Time to release yourself from the idea that you have to fight your way through life.

July 27: Sun coupled with North Node in Leo

Your original potential is totally visible and bringing itself to you. "Get on the horse and ride."

Sunday	Monday	Tuesday	Wednesday	Thursday	Friday	Saturday
1 ♂♄♃♇♆℞ ☽V/C 3:55 PM 7. Learning expands options.	**2** ♂♄♃♇♆℞ ☽→♓ 10:30 AM 8. Abundance is yours.	**3** ♂♄♃♇♆℞ 9. Spiritual renewal is activated.	**4** ♂♄⚷♃♇♆℞ Independence Day ☽-V/C 2:46 AM ☽→♈ 9:49 PM ⚷℞-2°♈25′- 9:46 PM 10. Inspiration transforms your day.	**5** ♂♄⚷♃♇♆℞ 2. Seek a harmonious decision.	**6** ♂♄⚷♃♇♆℞ 3. A creative shift occurs, have fun.	**7** ♂♄⚷♃♇♆℞ ☽-V/C 12:08 AM ☽→♉ 5:50 AM 4. Use your organizational skills.
8 ♂♄⚷♃♇♆℞ 5. Variety eases change.	**9** ♂♄⚷♃♇♆℞ ☽-V/C 9:09 AM ☽→♊ 9:58 AM ♀→♍ 7:33 PM 6. Focus on health and healing.	**10** ♂♄⚷♇♆℞ ☽-V/C 12:59 PM ♃D-13°♏20′ - 10:04 AM 7. Use your depth of knowledge.	**11** ♂♄⚷♇♆℞ ▼ ☽→♋ 10:58 AM 8. Life is abundantly new daily.	**12** ♂♄⚷♇♆℞ ▼ ● 20°♋41′ - 7:47 PM ☽-V/C 7:47 PM Solar Eclipse 20°♋50′ 8:01 PM 9. Heartfelt action is valued.	**13** ♂♄⚷♇♆℞ ☽→♌ 10:30 AM 10. Need an upgrade? Do it today.	**14** ♂⚷♄♇♆℞ ☽-V/C 4:11 PM 2. Trust your intuition.
15 ♂♄⚷♇♆℞ ☽→♍ 10:30 AM 3. Play fully and completely.	**16** ♂♄⚷♇♆℞ 4. All sides count equally.	**17** ♂♄⚷♇♆℞ ☽-V/C 3:49 AM ☽→♎ 12:42 PM 5. Clear your mind with a walk.	**18** ♂♄⚷♇♆℞ 6. Invite a friend to lunch.	**19** ♂♄⚷♇♆℞ ☽-V/C 12:52 PM ☽→♏ 6:12 PM 7. Do research on a new interest.	**20** ♂♄⚷♃♇♆℞ 8. Your value is priceless.	**21** ♂♄⚷♇♆℞ 9. The spiritually strong get involved.
22 ♂♄♇♆℞ ☽-V/C 2:17 AM ☽→♐ 3:12 AM ☉→♌ - 2:01 PM 10. Ignoring the past is a choice.	**23** ♂♄♇♆℞ 2. See both sides of an issue.	**24** ♂♄♇♆℞ ▲ ☽-V/C 1:21 AM ☽→♑ 2:48 PM 3. Find joy in all you do.	**25** ☿♂♄⚷♇♆℞ ▲ ☿℞-23°♌27′ - 10:03 PM 4. A solid foundation is required.	**26** ☿♂♄⚷♇♆℞ ☽-V/C 6:41 AM 5. Explore, be adventurous.	**27** ☿♂♄⚷♇♆℞ ○ 4°♒45′ - 1:20 PM ☽→♒ 3:40 AM Lunar Eclipse 4°♒45′ 1:21 PM 6. Make your home cozy.	**28** ☿♂♄⚷♇♆℞ 7. Expand your knowledge.
29 ☿♂♄⚷♇♆℞ ☽-V/C 2:24 AM ☽→♓ 4:27 PM 8. Ambition is a tool for success.	**30** ☿♂♄⚷♇♆℞ 9. Have compassion for humanity.	**31** ☿♂♄⚷♇♆℞ ☽-V/C 3:41 PM 10. Find a new beginning.				

♈ Aries	♍ Virgo	♓ Pisces	♃ Jupiter	→ Enters	2. Balance	8. Money
♉ Taurus	♎ Libra	☉ Sun	♄ Saturn	℞ Retrograde	3. Fun	9. Spirituality
♊ Gemini	♏ Scorpio	☽ Moon	♅ Uranus	S/D Stationary Direct	4. Structure	10. Visionary
♋ Cancer	♐ Sagittarius	☿ Mercury	♆ Neptune	V/C Void-of-Course	5. Action	11. Completion
♌ Leo	♑ Capricorn	♀ Venus	♇ Pluto	▲ Super Sensitivity	6. Love	
	♒ Aquarius	♂ Mars	⚷ Chiron	▼ Low Vitality	7. Learning	

New Moon in Cancer

When the Sun is in Cancer

It is now time to build our structure and foundation. Cancer holds the wisdom of the Great Cosmic Architect. Her statement is, "I build a lighted house and therein I dwell." The key is to use the materials of light, love, and wisdom to build your house and become the creator of form. Look within to see what lights your home and your body. Also check security systems, early environmental training, and mother/child relationships to see what materials you are using to build the structure for your life. Use this creating moon to build the structure you want.

Cancer Goddess

Hecate is a household goddess who assists people at times of transitions, such as childbirth and death. She is depicted as holding a torch to light the way when you reach major crossroads in life. Associated with the Underworld and the bridge into death and rebirth, Hecate is often shown with three heads and a loyal dog at her side. Her ability to see through the veil of illusion allowed her to assist Demeter in her search for Persephone, because Hecate could see into Hades. She rules over the earth, sea, and sky.

Are you, or someone in your household, feeling restless or aimless? Call upon Hecate's ability to clear the pathway through discernment, the wisdom that comes with age, and the knowledge of cycles.

Build Your Altar

Colors	Shades of gray, milky/creamy colors
Numerology	9 – Heartfelt action is valued
Tarot Card	Chariot – The ability to move forward, victory through action
Gemstones	Pearl, moonstone, ruby
Plant Remedy	Shooting Star – The ability to move straight ahead
Fragrance	Peppermint – The essence of the Great Mother

Moon Notes

July 12th, 7:47 PM
Solar Eclipse

New Moon 20° Cancer 41'
New Moons are about manifestation, planting seeds, and becoming fruitful.

Statement	I Feel
Body	Stomach
Mind	Worry
Spirit	Nurturing

Element
Water – Taking the path of least resistance, going with the flow, creativity at its best. Secretive, psychic, magnetic, glamourous, sensual, actress, escape artist, and healer.

Dropping Moon
Write your intentions early, before the Moon goes void.

Choice Points
Light	Cultural awareness
Shadow	Overly dramatic
Wisdom	Find clarity away from drama.

Sabian Symbol
A famous singer is proving her virtuosity during an operatic performance.

Potential
An unreasonable demand for observation of talent.

7th House Moon I Balance/I Feel

Umbrella Energy
One-on-one relationships, your people attraction, and how you work in relationships with the people you attract.

Karmic Awakening
Virgo/Pisces – Natural healing versus allopathic healing.

Cancer Victories & Challenges

Say all of the statements in this section out loud. Then, underline the phrase that means the most to you. Use the phrase as your affirmation for recalibrating throughout this moon phase.

Today I take advantage of my ability to take action and position myself for success. I clearly know that the road to success is before me, and all I need to do is move forward. I am aware that when I take action and move forward, the Universe fills in the dots. Whether I move left, right, or straight ahead doesn't matter—what matters is movement. Today, I release the indecisiveness that keeps me stuck. Today, I let go of vacillation that exhausts my mind. Today, I take my foot off of the brakes and find the gas pedal. I allow movement to occur, even if I don't know where I am going. When I take action, I trust that guideposts will appear. I am aware that action leads me to my new direction. So, today I know and GO! I remember that Karma comes to the space of non-action, while success comes through action. Action brings me to my victory. Standing still leads to regret, resentment, and chaos.

I am aware that action can be as simple as taking a walk on the beach, buying fresh flowers to add a new dimension to my home, or simply going to a new restaurant for lunch. I take action today to break up a crystallized pattern and, in so doing, my life begins to show me newfound awareness and light to guide me.

Cancer Homework

Cancers manifest best when catering, writing cookbooks, in marriage and family counseling, providing childcare, giving massage, or when engaged in genealogy, arts and crafts, architecture, and home-building.

During the Cancer new moon cycle, we are asked to create light into form and turn it into beauty on four levels. Physically, we must feel nurtured and protected. Emotionally, we must set safe boundaries for the expression of our feelings. Mentally, we must release self-pity and embrace rightful thinking. Spiritually, we must hold the space for the infusion of light to shine inside all bodies on Earth.

Victory List

Acknowledge what you have overcome.
Keep this list active during this moon cycle.
Honoring victory allows you to accept success.

Sky Power Yoga

Child's Pose

You need two bath towels and one to two pillows for the prop.

Fold the two towels in half lengthwise, roll them into a log, and place them on the floor. Put both pillows on top of the rolled towels to support you in the pose.

Begin kneeling, placing your support prop in front of your knees then come onto hands and knees. Align your knees under your hips and your hands under your shoulders.

Close your eyes. Breathe in and out slowly and deeply several times through your nose with your awareness on your stomach.

Exhale and drop your hips back towards your heels so your front torso lowers onto the support prop. Slide your hands forward slightly and rest your head on the support prop.

Turn your head to whichever side is most comfortable.

Inhale deeply. Exhale slowly as you say or think to yourself the mantra *I Feel*.

Relax fully into the support prop and the pose. Remain with the mantra and breath as long as desired.

Manifesting List

Cancer Manifesting Ideas

Now is the time to focus on manifesting being a good mother, new ways to be a mom, nurturing and self-love, the ability to see joy, a clutter-free home, your dream home, and inner and outer security.

This or something better than this comes to me in an easy and pleasurable way, for the good of all concerned. Thank you, Universe!

New Moon in Cancer

Your Personal Moon Experience

Fill in the Cosmic Check-In page. Then look up the degree of the Moon on the chart below. Take note of the "I" statement on the outside of the wheel where the Moon is located. Now, locate the same degree on your own chart and make a note of the house and corresponding "I" statement. Go back to the Cosmic Check-In page and circle the two statements from the charts and read what you wrote. This will give you an idea about what to expect from this moon phase on a personal level. For more information on personalizing your *Moon Book*, go to www.BlueMoonAcademy.com and look for *How to Use the Moon Book*.

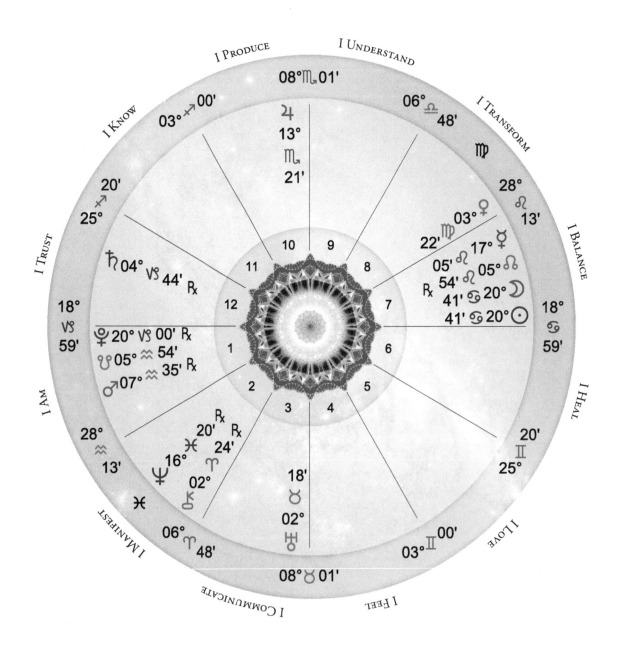

♈ Aries	♋ Cancer	♏ Scorpio	♓ Pisces	♀ Venus	♅ Uranus	☊ North Node
♉ Taurus	♌ Leo	♐ Sagittarius	☉ Sun	♂ Mars	♆ Neptune	☋ South Node
♊ Gemini	♍ Virgo	♑ Capricorn	☽ Moon	♃ Jupiter	♇ Pluto	℞ Retrograde
	♎ Libra	♒ Aquarius	☿ Mercury	♄ Saturn	⚷ Chiron	

Cosmic Check-in

Cancer New Moon
July 12th, 7:47 PM
Solar Eclipse

Take a moment to write a brief phrase for each "I" statement.
This activates all areas of your life for this creative cycle.

♋ I Feel

♌ I Love

♍ I Heal

♎ I Balance

♏ I Transform

♐ I Understand

♑ I Produce

♒ I Know

♓ I Trust

♈ I Am

♉ I Manifest

♊ I Communicate

Full Moon in Aquarius

When the Sun is Opposite the Moon

Full moons are always in opposition to the Sun. This creates a feeling of tension between where you want to shine and how your feelings are flowing on a sensory level about the Sun's directive. The two forces seem like they are working against each other, yet they are on the same team displaying different techniques to obtain the same mission. The Aquarian/Leo polarity creates tension between the quest for group interaction and the recognition of self.

Aquarius Goddess

The Egyptian Goddess Maat ushers in a time of discovery about who you are at the core, as your most balanced and beneficent self, and about the work you came here to do in this lifetime. According to the Egyptian Book of the Dead, Maat is the goddess you visit upon your death. She places her single ostrich feather on the scale to be weighed against your heart. If you have lived a virtuous life, and reached your highest potential as a kind and decent human being, your heart will be as light as Maat's feather, and you would cross over. If not, you will be devoured by the Goddess Ammit and would be reborn into duality for another lifetime.

Let this moon show you your potential and re-orient yourself to your life's highest work and purpose. The Egyptian word for heart was "ib." Ask yourself, who will "I be" in this lifetime?

Build Your Altar

Colors Electric colors, neon, multi-colors, pearl white

Numerology 6 – Make your home cozy

Tarot Card Star – Being guided by a higher source

Gemstones Aquamarine, amethyst, opal

Plant remedy Queen of the Night Cactus – The ability to see in the dark

Fragrance Myrrh – Healing the nervous system

Moon Notes

July 27th, 1:20 PM
Lunar Eclipse

Full Moon 4° Aquarius 45'
   Full Moons are about releasing, letting go, becoming free, and recalibrating.

Statement I Know

Body Ankles

Mind True genius

Spirit Vision

Element
   Air – The breath of life that allows the mind to achieve new insights and fresh perspectives, inspiration, active and abstract dreaming, and freedom from attachments.

Choice Points
   Light   Integrity
   Shadow   Conservatism
   Wisdom   How your thoughts affect the environment.

Sabian Symbol
   A council of ancestors is seen implementing the efforts of a young leader.

Potential
   A reminder that all information is available to us through our spiritual practice.

3rd House Moon I Communicate/I Know

Umbrella Energy
   How you get the word out and the message behind the words.

Clearing the Slate

Sixty hours before the full moon negative traits connected to the astro-sign might become activated to trigger what needs to be released during the full moon phase. You may notice yourself becoming stubborn, escaping reality by living in the future, and the need to be rebellious if you feel frenzied or chaotic. Make a list, look in the mirror, and for each negative trait, tell yourself *I am sorry, I forgive you, thank you for your awareness,* and *I love you.*

Aquarius Victories & Challenges

Say all of the statements in this section out loud. Then, underline the phrase that means the most to you. Use the phrase as your affirmation for recalibrating throughout this moon phase.

Today my true potential can be realized. All I have to do is take a risk and know that my faith is in operation. My future is very bright and offers me a promise of things to come. Today is a day of destiny. I have chosen this day to determine a DESTINY PROMISE I MADE TO MYSELF BEFORE I CAME INTO THIS LIFE. All that is required of me is to move out of my comfort zone and take a risk. I am aware that faith cannot be determined without risk. I take the risk to move into the next space of creation in my life. I release fear and move into faith, knowing full well that my logic and reason are part of the fear that keeps me stuck.

I am reminded that the kingdom of heaven is open to the child. I find the child within me today to embrace what life has for me with open arms and a spirit of adventure. I know my true potential lives inside my magical child and she/he is willing to play and go for the gusto. I am here in this life to fulfill my promise to experience life to the fullest and to release the fear of judgment that has hounded me and kept me from playing full-out. I remember that when I experience, I gather a knowledge base within my Soul and keep my agreement with myself and the Universe. I connect to my super-consciousness and take on the bigger view of my life and all that it has to offer me when I risk reason and take a leap of faith. I know in the depth of my awareness that, if I jump off the diving board, there will be water in the pool. I am willing to risk reason for an experience. Everything I ever wanted is one step outside my comfort zone. I go for the GUSTO today! I release my fear today and turn it into faith. I trust in the promise of things to come. I know my potential is realized today, and that all I have to do is say "YES!" to life!

Aquarius Homework

The Aquarius moon reminds us of our connection to solar fire (the heart of the Sun) also known as the Heart of the Cosmos. During this time, we get our vitality recharged and our potent power comes into play motivating the masses to receive more energy to transmute into the new world. Voice all that you know to be true to the point of self-realization where your authentic purpose can be revealed to you. This is the moment where you have released all that has kept you from your true sense of freedom. Remember to replenish all the electrolytes in your system.

Gratitude List

Keep this list active throughout the moon cycle. This will bring you to a level of completion so that a new cycle of opportunity can occur in your life. Be prepared for miracles!

I am thankful for the path of my life – it has brought me to now. I am ready for the next chapter & what ever the path is. I am thankful for me & I'm ready to appreciate all of me

Sky Power Yoga

Seated Ankle Rotations

You need one chair for the prop.

Sit in a chair with your back straight and your feet on the floor, hip-width apart. Feet should have solid contact with the floor. Use pillows or folded towels to support your feet, if necessary.

Rest your right ankle on your lower left thigh. Lace the fingers of your left hand between your right foot's toes. Your pinky finger goes between your outer two toes and so forth until your index finger is next to your big toe.

Relax. Close your eyes. Breathe in and out slowly and deeply several times through your nose with your awareness on the ankle.

Inhale deeply. Say or think the mantra *I Know*.

Exhale slowly while using your hand to guide the ball of your foot in a circular motion, counterclockwise. Repeat as many times as feels comfortable and then switch to the other foot.

Freedom List

Say this statement out loud three times before writing your list:

I am a free spiritual being and it is my desire to be free to think and to express myself fully.

Aquarius
Recalibrating Ideas

Now is the time to activate a game change in my life, and give up resistance to authority figures, blocks to living in the moment, unnecessary rebellion, non-productive frenzy and fantasy, the need to be spontaneous, and people who aren't team players.

Freedom is mine when I live my truth!

145

Full Moon in Aquarius

Your Personal Moon Experience

Fill in the Cosmic Check-In page. Then look up the degree of the Moon on the chart below. Take note of the "I" statement on the outside of the wheel where the Moon is located. Now, locate the same degree on your own chart and make

a note of the house and corresponding "I" statement. Go back to the Cosmic Check-In page, circle the two statements from the charts, and read what you wrote. This will give you an idea about what to expect from this moon phase on a personal level. For a personalized *My Moon Experience* Astrology reading with Beatrex, go to www.beatrex.com.

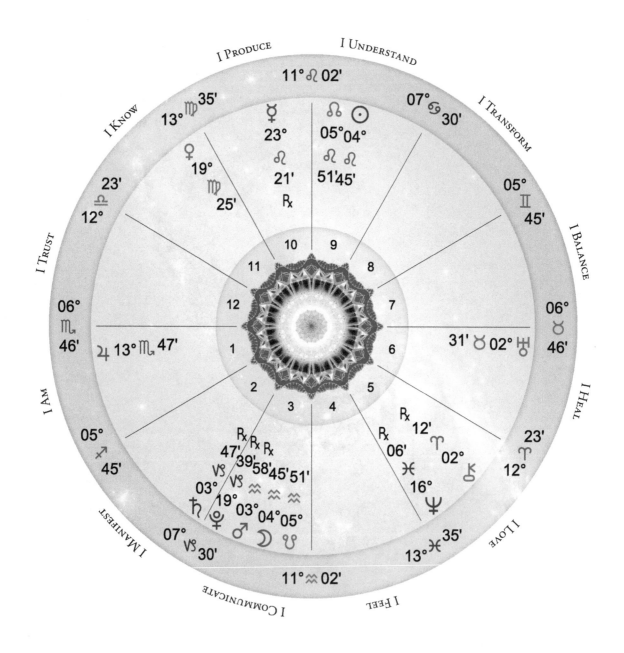

♈ Aries	♋ Cancer	♏ Scorpio	♓ Pisces	♀ Venus	♅ Uranus	☊ North Node
♉ Taurus	♌ Leo	♐ Sagittarius	☉ Sun	♂ Mars	♆ Neptune	☋ South Node
♊ Gemini	♍ Virgo	♑ Capricorn	☽ Moon	♃ Jupiter	♇ Pluto	℞ Retrograde
	♎ Libra	♒ Aquarius	☿ Mercury	♄ Saturn	⚷ Chiron	

Cosmic Check-in

Aquarius Full Moon
July 27th, 1:20 PM
Lunar Eclipse

Take a moment to write a brief phrase for each "I" statement.
This activates all areas of your life for this creative cycle.

♒ I Know

♓ I Trust

♈ I Am

♉ I Manifest

♊ I Communicate

♋ I Feel

♌ I Love

♍ I Heal

♎ I Balance

♏ I Transform

♐ I Understand

♑ I Produce

August

August 1-11: Mars conjunct South Node in Aquarius

Urges for unconventional or unusual sexual attraction could occur that you may regret later. It works best when letting the mind have the sex. Taking into consideration the 'been there, done that' South Node influence, the best way to work this is to keep it in the mind.

August 6: Venus enters Libra

Expect an advancement in the standard of morality. This is a great time for diplomacy. Have great expectations regarding partnership.

August 6-7: Low Vitality

If expectations are high and immediate gratification gets involved, you may experience total burnout. Slow down, get rest, and drink lots of water.

August 7: Uranus retrograde in Taurus until 2019

Obsessing about the future will exhaust you. Set your intentions before this date and be clear. This way, the Law of Direction will carry you through this long-range challenge. Another option is to use this transit is to complete unfinished business.

August 11: Mercury, Sun, and Moon tripled in Leo

Get your mind clear about your love intentions. Your inner and outer expression are integrated, however, your mind could play havoc if you are not clear.

August 12: Mars enters Capricorn

Success and victory are here and can take you to the top of the mountain right now. Create an action list and focus on success.

August 18: Mercury goes direct in Leo

Make love songs a part of your day. Love is in your thought wave. Ride the wave and speak with your heart-mind, and bliss will manifest. Live love every day.

August 19-20: Super Sensitivity

Pay attention to what is in mass-consciousness thinking and avoid it. Just because it is in popular culture right now, do what you can to press your 'ignore button' and stay away. It is toxic and will bring on a depression.

August 22: Sun enters Virgo

The mind becomes active and has a tendency to go overboard, shrinking everything into a detail. What is best here is to use your mind to give birth to divinity and raise the standard of excellence.

August 27: Mars direct in Capricorn

All action leads to success and victory here. You become aware of your path to success and become unstoppable.

Sunday	Monday	Tuesday	Wednesday	Thursday	Friday	Saturday
			1 ☿♂ ♄⚷♇♆℞ ☽→♈ 3:54 AM 2. Stay in balance.	**2** ☿♂ ♄⚷♇♆℞ ☽-V/C 7:52 PM 3. Base your choice on fun.	**3** ☿♂ ♄⚷♇♆℞ ☽→♉ 12:50 PM 4. Set the ground-work for victory.	**4** ☿♂ ♄⚷♇♆℞ 5. Adapt to changing needs.
5 ☿♂ ♄⚷♇♆℞ ☽-V/C 4:46 PM ☽→♊ 6:31 PM 6. Stay healthy by walking.	**6** ☿♂ ♄⚷♇♆℞ ▼ ♀→♎ - 4:29 PM 7. Let knowledge bring in your wealth.	**7** ☿♂ ♄♅⚷♇♆℞ ▼ ☽-V/C 12:54 AM ☽→♋ 9:00 PM ♅SR-2°♉33′ - 9:50 AM 8. Increase the flow by being outrageous.	**8** ☿♂ ♄♅⚷♇♆℞ 10. A new day is a new beginning.	**9** ☿♂ ♄♅⚷♇♆℞ ☽-V/C 4:20 AM ☽→♌ 9:17 PM 2. Keep steady; intuition is your guide.	**10** ☿♂ ♄♅⚷♇♆℞ 3. Optimism opens the door.	**11** ☿♂ ♄♅⚷♇♆℞ ● 18°♌42′ - 2:57 AM ☽-V/C 2:57 AM ☽→♍ 8:58 PM Solar Eclipse 18°♌35′ 2:46 AM 4. Dependable people appear today.
12 ☿♂ ♄♅⚷♇♆℞ ♂→♑ 7:15 PM 5. Constant variety adds zest to your life.	**13** ☿♂ ♄♅⚷♇♆℞ ☽-V/C 9:37 PM ☽→♎ 9:57 PM 6. Light incense and bring in flowers.	**14** ☿♂ ♄♅⚷♇♆℞ 7. Share your wisdom.	**15** ☿♂ ♄♅⚷♇♆℞ 8. Lead to increase the wealth of others.	**16** ☿♂ ♄♅⚷♇♆℞ ☽-V/C 12:55 AM ☽→♏ 1:54 AM 9. Trust Divine Intelligence.	**17** ☿♂ ♄♅⚷♇♆℞ 10. Let your future vision be a motivator.	**18** ♂ ♄♅⚷♇♆℞ ☽-V/C 8:06 AM ☽→♐ 9:44 AM ☿SD-11°♌32′ - 9:26 PM 11. The Universe has your back.
19 ♂ ♄♅⚷♇♆℞ ▲ 3. See a movie that will make you laugh.	**20** ♂ ♄♅⚷♇♆℞ ▲ ☽-V/C 4:46 PM ☽→♑ 9:00 PM 4. Create an efficient plan of action.	**21** ♂ ♄♅⚷♇♆℞ 5. Seek variety and open new pathways.	**22** ♂ ♄♅⚷♇♆℞ ☉→♍ 9:10 PM 6. Healthy choices make healthy bodies.	**23** ♂ ♄♅⚷♇♆℞ ☽-V/C 7:18 AM ☽→♒ 9:55 AM 7. Your knowledge has the answers.	**24** ♂ ♄♅⚷♇♆℞ ☽-V/C 9:38 PM 8. Allow abundance in.	**25** ♂ ♄♅⚷♇♆℞ ☽→♓ 10:32 PM 9. Pray with passion.
26 ♂ ♄♅⚷♇♆℞ ○ 3°♓12′ - 4:56 AM 10. Follow the light, it knows where to go.	**27** ♄♅⚷♇♆℞ ♂SD-28°♑36′ 7:06 AM 2. Keep a steady grip.	**28** ♄♅⚷♇♆℞ ☽-V/C 6:54 AM ☽→♈ 9:35 AM 3. Become joy in the present.	**29** ♄♅⚷♇♆℞ 4. Remember synergy is the answer.	**30** ♄♅⚷♇♆℞ ☽-V/C 4:03 PM ☽→♉ 6:30 PM 5. Plan a quick getaway trip.	**31** ♄♅⚷♇♆℞ 6. Bring your love their favorite treat.	

♈ Aries	♍ Virgo	♓ Pisces	♃ Jupiter	➡ Enters	2. Balance	8. Money
♉ Taurus	♎ Libra	☉ Sun	♄ Saturn	℞ Retrograde	3. Fun	9. Spirituality
♊ Gemini	♏ Scorpio	☽ Moon	♅ Uranus	S/D Stationary Direct	4. Structure	10. Visionary
♋ Cancer	♐ Sagittarius	☿ Mercury	♆ Neptune	V/C Void-of-Course	5. Action	11. Completion
♌ Leo	♑ Capricorn	♀ Venus	♇ Pluto	▲ Super Sensitivity	6. Love	
	♒ Aquarius	♂ Mars	⚷ Chiron	▼ Low Vitality	7. Learning	

New Moon in Leo

When the Sun is in Leo

This is the time when you feel the power from the Sun, the heart of the Cosmos. Leo has a direct relationship with the Sun's heart. The Sun rules your identity. Now is the time to shine and stand tall in the center of your life. Allow yourself to feel the power of your individual conscious Self. When you align with the power of the Sun, you become radiant. This radiance gives you the power to transmit energy into life. Personal fulfillment becomes a reality when you align your will with love. Remember to live love every day!

Leo Goddess

Aphrodite sashays into the Summer party, full of moxie and ready to flirt! The Goddess of Beauty and Love is enlivening all aspects of your life with joyful play!

Get into your Feminine Light. Giggle, dance, and sing! What a great time for a girl's night out or karaoke on the beach beside a roaring bonfire! Work it! Swish your skirts and strut your stuff! Tap into Aphrodite's inner light for fun and frolic. Aphrodite reminds us that play is also our spiritual work. Bring some joy and fun into it!

Build Your Altar

Colors	Royal purple, royal blue, orange
Numerology	4 – Dependable people appear
Tarot Card	Sun – To stand tall in the center of life
Gemstones	Peridot, emerald, amber
Plant Remedy	Sunflower – Standing tall in the center of your garden
Fragrance	Jasmine – Remembering your Soul's original intention

Moon Notes

August 11th, 2:57 AM
Solar Eclipse

New Moon 18° Leo 42'
New moons are about manifestation, planting seeds, and becoming fruitful.

Statement	I Love
Body	Heart
Mind	Self-confidence
Spirit	Generosity

Element
Fire – Igniting, dissolving, accelerating, cleansing, advancing awareness, impatience, leadership, passion, and vitality.

Dropping Moon
Write your intentions early, before the Moon goes void.

Choice Points
Light	Breaking routine
Shadow	Restricted space
Wisdom	Seek new experiences with the realms that stretch the fabric of the usual.

Sabian Symbol
A houseboat party.

Potential
Joining with others in a spiritual adventure.

2nd House Moon   I Manifest/I Love

Umbrella Energy
The way you make your money and the way you spend your money.

Karmic Awakening
Scorpio/Taurus – My money or our money?

Leo Victories & Challenges

Say all of the statements in this section out loud. Then, underline the phrase that means the most to you. Use the phrase as your affirmation for recalibrating throughout this moon phase.

Today, I am at the center of bliss, happiness, abundance, and total celebration. It is my time to shine and feel the power of my true self blasting the Universe, the entire planet, and all of life with the light of my awareness. There is nothing that can stop me today, because I am free to be me. When I am free to be me, I can stand naked in the daylight and have nothing to hide. I truly know that all of life loves me and I love all of life. I feel the radiance and vibration of my being activating me with aliveness, vitality, and charisma. I know that I can make a difference because I celebrate life by infusing, sparking, and igniting matter with light. I am open and ready to embrace all that comes to me with joy. I say "YES!" to all opportunities today; knowing that today is my day. I am in the flow of abundance and I let abundance flow through me.

The child within me is open and ready to play full out; there is not a cloud in the sky today that can eclipse me or place a shadow on me and keep me from my true level of power. I am aware that the child state of being within me simply says yes to action and action is power. When I take action today, my possibilities are endless because they are generated from my true self and motivated by happiness, joy, and freedom. The child within me is able to play full out because I have birthed myself beyond my old perception of blocks. I know that in taking this true power, to be motivated by happiness, pathways on all levels and in all dimensions can open to the empowerment of joy. Empowerment is mine today because I am shining from within myself and I know my deepest self is connected to the source. Empowerment occurs when I live from the inside out. Today, I wave the banner of my being from within, feel the glow, and go.

Leo Homework

Leos manifest best through fashion and jewelry design, glamour, politics, super-modeling, movie stardom, child advocacy, fundraising, toy and game design, image consulting, authoring children's books, sales, and cardiology.

Leo gets you closer to your essential self, reminding you of your Soul's original intention. You become ready to receive the benefits of reflective light and radiating light at the same time, so that you can see your personality and your Soul connecting to love which constitutes a new level of fulfillment. Expect purification, transmutation, communication, and mastery to be part of your personal experience.

Victory List

Acknowledge what you have overcome.
Keep this list active during this moon cycle.
Honoring victory allows you to accept success.

Sky Power Yoga

Seated Cactus Arms

You need one chair for the prop.

Sit one hand-width forward from the chair back with your feet on the floor hip-width apart. Feet should have solid contact with the floor. Use pillows or folded towels to support your feet, if necessary.

Lengthen your spine to straighten your back. To make the cactus arms, lift

and bend arms so that your hands are at a 90 degree angle from your elbow.

Relax and close your eyes. Breathe in and out slowly and deeply several times through your nose

maintaining your awareness on your heart center.

Inhale deeply and squeeze your shoulder blades together, then press elbows back, and lift your sternum slightly. Say or think to yourself the mantra *I Love*.

Exhale slowly. Bring your elbows together and round your back slightly. Your body does a subtle back bend as you inhale and a subtle forward bend as you exhale. Repeat as desired.

Manifesting List

Leo
Manifesting Ideas

Now is the time to focus on manifesting new love or new ways of loving, new creative ways of expressing myself, bonding with those I love, quality time with those I love, knowledge of my Soul's intention, fun with my children, being a bright beaming light, and connecting to the hearts of humanity.

This or something better than this comes to me in an easy and pleasurable way, for the good of all concerned. Thank you, Universe!

155

New Moon in Leo

Your Personal Moon Experience

Fill in the Cosmic Check-In page. Then look up the degree of the Moon on the chart below. Take note of the "I" statement on the outside of the wheel where the Moon is located. Now, locate the same degree on your own chart and make a note of the house and corresponding "I" statement. Go back to the Cosmic Check-In page and circle the two statements from the charts and read what you wrote. This will give you an idea about what to expect from this moon phase on a personal level. For more information on personalizing your *Moon Book*, go to www.BlueMoonAcademy.com and look for *How to Use the Moon Book*.

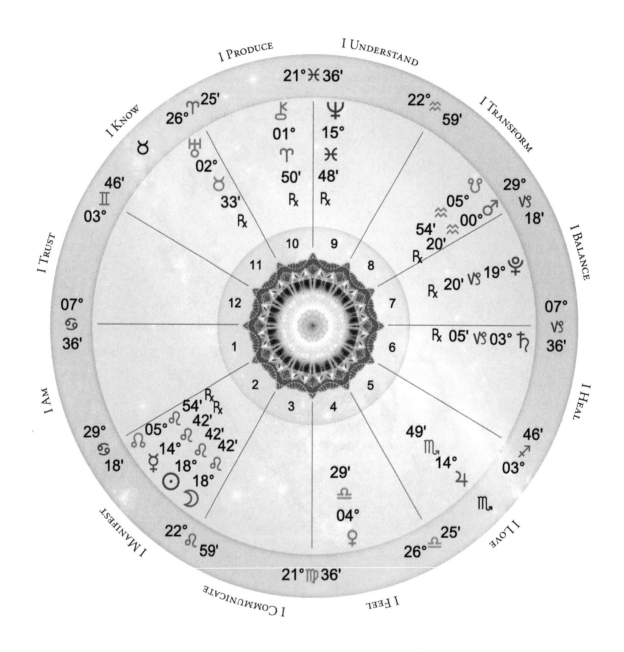

♈ Aries	♋ Cancer	♏ Scorpio	♓ Pisces	♀ Venus	♅ Uranus	☊ North Node
♉ Taurus	♌ Leo	♐ Sagittarius	☉ Sun	♂ Mars	♆ Neptune	☋ South Node
♊ Gemini	♍ Virgo	♑ Capricorn	☽ Moon	♃ Jupiter	♇ Pluto	℞ Retrograde
	♎ Libra	♒ Aquarius	☿ Mercury	♄ Saturn	⚷ Chiron	

Cosmic Check-in

Leo New Moon
August 11th, 2:57 AM
Solar Eclipse

Take a moment to write a brief phrase for each "I" statement.
This activates all areas of your life for this creative cycle.

♌ I Love

♍ I Heal

♎ I Balance

♏ I Transform

♐ I Understand

♑ I Produce

♒ I Know

♓ I Trust

♈ I Am

♉ I Manifest

♊ I Communicate

♋ I Feel

Full Moon in Pisces

When the Sun is Opposite the Moon

Full moons are always in opposition to the Sun. This creates a feeling of tension between where you want to shine and how your feelings are flowing on a sensory level about the Sun's directive. The two forces seem like they are working against each other, yet they are on the same team displaying different techniques to obtain the same mission. The Pisces/Virgo polarity creates tension between addiction and perfection.

Pisces Goddess

Lady Change'e, the Chinese Moon Goddess, is honored at the full moon closest to the Autumnal Equinox, with the sharing of moon cakes, whose round shape symbolizes completeness and togetherness. She ascended to the Moon after drinking the Elixir of Immortality. It had been gifted to her husband after he slew nine out of ten wayward sons of an emperor who had turned into suns and were scorching the Earth. If she and her husband had split the elixir, they would each be immortal, but her mistake in drinking it all (or her sacrifice, depending on the telling) means she will spend eternity on the Moon.

Depicted with a companion rabbit, a magical potion maker, Change'e is beneficent, and will grant your wishes, but remember she favors those who are careful what they wish for, and who take initiative towards working to make their own dreams a reality. Trust in the process of transformation, like the changing colors of the leaves, but also put both of your feet firmly on the path towards wholeness.

Build Your Altar

Colors	Greens, blues, amethyst, aquamarine
Numerology	10 – Follow the light, it knows where to go
Tarot Card	The Hanged Man – Learning to let go
Gemstones	Opal, turquoise, amethyst
Plant remedy	Passion flower – The ability to live in the here and now
Fragrance	White lotus – Connecting to the Divine without arrogance

Moon Notes

August 26th, 4:56 AM

Full Moon 3° Pisces 12'
Full Moons are about releasing, letting go, becoming free, and recalibrating.

Statement	I Trust
Body	Feet
Mind	Super-sensitive
Spirit	Mystical

Element
Water – Taking the path of least resistance, going with the flow, and creativity at it's best. Secretive, psychic, magnetic, glamourous, sensual, actress, escape artist, and healer.

Choice Points
Light   Defragmentation
Shadow   Gridlock
Wisdom   Start over, fresh and new.

Sabian Symbol
Heavy car traffic on a narrow isthmus linking two seashore resorts.

Potential
Everything is going your way even if you are in the wrong lane.

7th House Moon   I Balance/I Trust

Umbrella Energy
One-on-one relationships. Your people attraction, and how you work in relationships with the people you attract.

Clearing the Slate

Sixty hours before the full moon negative traits connected to the astro-sign might become activated to trigger what needs to be released during the full moon phase. You may notice a sudden urge to escape into unrealistic attitudes or addictive habits that bring a feeling of aimlessness. Make a list, look in the mirror, and for each negative trait, tell yourself *I am sorry, I forgive you, thank you for your awareness,* and *I love you.*

Pisces Victories & Challenges

Say all of the statements in this section out loud. Then, underline the phrase that means the most to you. Use the phrase as your affirmation for recalibrating throughout this moon phase.

The best thing I can do for myself today is to get out of the way, so life can take its own course without the interference of my control drama. I take time out to let go and let things be. I have become too involved in the details and have lost sight of the vastness of the Universe, and the infinite possibilities that are available to me at all times and in every moment. I am aware that all I need is a different way of seeing what I have perceived as a problem, and that my view is limited by my needs, rather than by accepting things as they are. I trust that, when I get out of the way and give space to the power of NOW, all is in Divine Order and everything works out for the good of all concerned. This is the day when doing nothing gets me everything. I allow myself to experience the void. I empty myself of my rigidity, small-mindedness, racing thoughts, the need to be right, and to control outcomes. I know that non-action will present me with right action. I give the Universe a chance and trust the view to be larger than mine. When I accept myself as I am, I learn what I can become. I remove myself from all of the mind chatter and allow for silence to do its work. I am aware that a quiet mind brings me peace (the absence of conflict). In turning upside down, I see how right-side-up things really are. Acceptance brings me perspective. Acceptance sets me free. Acceptance brings me wholeness. Acceptance widens my mind.

Pisces Homework

Get a foot massage to bring your energy back to the ground. Feel the power of your path on the bottom of your feet. Now that you are back to your body, it is time to make a list of the ways your boundaries get breached. After the completion of your list, read it out loud and then throw it in the ocean.

Gratitude List

Keep this list active throughout the moon cycle. This will bring you to a level of completion so that a new cycle of opportunity can occur in your life. Be prepared for miracles!

Sky Power Yoga

Rocky Mountain Pose

No props are needed.

Stand with your feet hip-width apart. Lift your toes and wiggle them for 30 seconds. Spreading your toes wide, place them back on the floor.

As you exhale, rock back and forth and side to side—massaging the bottoms of your feet. Feel yourself grounded, stable, and strong amidst movement.

Settle into mountain pose. Squeeze your thighs to lift your kneecaps. Slightly tuck your tailbone down and feel your hips align over your ankles.

Lengthen your spine. Roll your shoulders back and down reaching your fingertips towards the floor. With your chest gently lifted from the sternum, turn your palms out slightly. To add support: imagine a strong line of vertical energy running from the bottom of your feet to the top of your head like a tree with strong roots running deep into the earth.

Relax. Close your eyes. Breathe in and out slowly and deeply several times through your nose with your awareness on your feet.

Inhale deeply as you say or think to yourself the mantra *I Trust.* As you exhale slowly, your exhalation roots you more deeply into the earth. Repeat as desired.

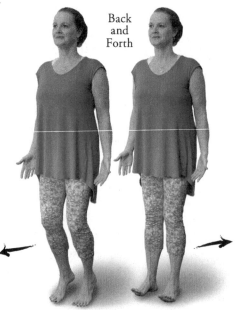

Back and Forth

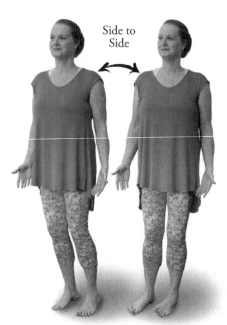

Side to Side

Freedom List

Say this statement out loud three times before writing your list:

I am a free spiritual being and it is my desire to be free to think and to express myself fully.

Pisces
Recalibrating Ideas

Now is the time to activate a game change in my life, and give up addictions, illusions and fantasy, escape dramas, martyrdom, victimhood, and mental chaos.

From this day forward I resolve to be true — first to myself and my highest self, and then to the highest self in me which is the Source of Love That I Am.

Full Moon in Pisces

Your Personal Moon Experience

Fill in the Cosmic Check-In page. Then look up the degree of the Moon on the chart below. Take note of the "I" statement on the outside of the wheel where the Moon is located. Now, locate the same degree on your own chart and make

a note of the house and corresponding "I" statement. Go back to the Cosmic Check-In page, circle the two statements from the charts, and read what you wrote. This will give you an idea about what to expect from this moon phase on a personal level. For a personalized *My Moon Experience* Astrology reading with Beatrex, go to www.beatrex.com.

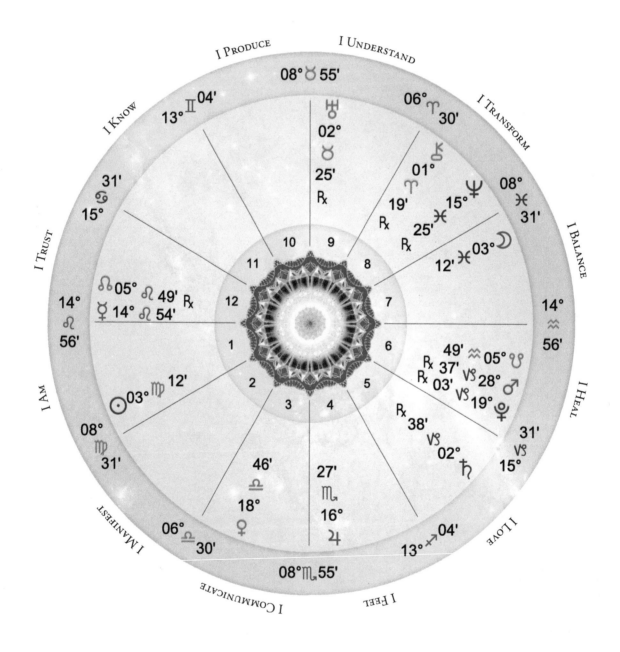

♈ Aries	♋ Cancer	♏ Scorpio	♓ Pisces	♀ Venus	♅ Uranus	☊ North Node
♉ Taurus	♌ Leo	♐ Sagittarius	☉ Sun	♂ Mars	♆ Neptune	☋ South Node
♊ Gemini	♍ Virgo	♑ Capricorn	☽ Moon	♃ Jupiter	♇ Pluto	℞ Retrograde
	♎ Libra	♒ Aquarius	☿ Mercury	♄ Saturn	⚷ Chiron	

Cosmic Check-in

Pisces Full Moon
August 26th
4:56 AM

Take a moment to write a brief phrase for each "I" statement.
This activates all areas of your life for this creative cycle.

♓ I Trust

♈ I Am

♉ I Manifest

♊ I Communicate

♋ I Feel

♌ I Love

♍ I Heal

♎ I Balance

♏ I Transform

♐ I Understand

♑ I Produce

♒ I Know

September

September 4-5: Low Vitality

Don't push the envelope, it may get you in trouble.

September 5: Mercury enters Virgo

Oh my, 'hold on to your hat'... your mind could be working overtime! This is not the time to make a decision. The 'windshield wipers of the mind' can make trouble if you try to decide which way to go.

September 6: Saturn goes direct in Capricorn

This calls for a champagne celebration. The stifling and oppression is over. Wide-range thinking is back in style. Feel the freedom from details and from determining what is wrong rather than allowing what is right to move you towards liberty. Guilt is no longer an issue. The heavy weight of the 'should' is over. Jiminy Cricket is on vacation for awhile.

September 9: Venus enters Scorpio

Get ready for great sex.

September 9: Uranus in Taurus opposite Venus in Scorpio

An unexpected windfall in business could happen. Keep your arms open in receiving mode.

September 10: Mars re-enters Aquarius

The element of surprise can be a part of this transit. Expect an expanded need to be original, free, and independent. Your progressive nature takes you to the top of any situation. Keep it going and you will find yourself in the middle of some amazing, innovative success.

September 17-18: Super Sensitivity

Keep your mind to yourself, in order to keep from being pulled into chaos.

September 21: Mercury enters Libra

Your mind is working overtime trying to connect. Stay balanced with beauty on your mind and your action will follow accordingly.

September 22: Sun enters Libra – Autumn Equinox

The idea of relating is becoming overwhelming. Work on refinement and all will be well.

September 24: Chiron and Moon conjunct in Aries opposite Mercury and Sun conjunct in Libra

The feminine struggle is evident here. Time to move beyond past perceptions and ask directly for what you want.

September 24: Mars and South Node conjunct in Aquarius

This is old news searching for a new way of evolving. You may find your perfect group to make the world a better place. Please check their commitment to avoid spending too much time with non-producers.

September 25: Chiron retrograde backs into Pisces

Time to review your relationship with God.

September 30: Pluto goes direct in Capricorn

Look for leftovers of unfinished business. Handle it and move on.

Sunday	Monday	Tuesday	Wednesday	Thursday	Friday	Saturday
						1 ♄♅⚷♇♆℞ ☽-V/C 10:56 PM 7. Get smart any way you choose.
2 ♄♅⚷♇♆℞ ☽→♊ 1:01 AM 8. Spend money and enjoy it.	**3** ♄♅⚷♇♆℞ Labor Day ☽-V/C 11:37 PM 9. Live a spiritually creative day.	**4** ♄♅⚷♇♆℞ ▼ ☽→♋ 5:03 AM 10. Never regret your extravagances.	**5** ♄♅⚷♇♆℞ ▼ ☿→♍ 7:40 PM 11. Be empowered by intuitive knowing.	**6** ♅⚷♇♆℞ ☽-V/C 5:42 AM ☽→♌ 6:54 AM ♄SD 2°♑32′ - 4:10 AM 3. Enjoy your creative flow.	**7** ♅⚷♇♆℞ 4. Is your situation supportive?	**8** ♅⚷♇♆℞ ☽-V/C 6:31 AM ☽→♍ 7:29 AM 5. Go on an adventure!
9 ♅⚷♇♆℞ ● 17°♍00′ - 11:01AM ♀→♏ 2:26 AM 6. Live love everyday.	**10** ♅⚷♇♆℞ Rosh Hashanah ☽-V/C 8:12 AM ☽→♎ 8:19 AM ♂→♒ 5:57 PM 7. Learn to trust your knowing.	**11** ♅⚷♇♆℞ ☽-V/C 3:57 PM 8. Use your wealth to bring more success.	**12** ♅⚷♇♆℞ ☽→♏ 11:14 AM 9. Pray intently for harmony.	**13** ♅⚷♇♆℞ 10. Live in the moment.	**14** ♅⚷♇♆℞ ☽-V/C 1:53 AM ☽→♐ 5:44 PM 2. Be adaptable.	**15** ♅⚷♇♆℞ 3. Be playful today.
16 ♅⚷♇♆℞ ☽-V/C 4:14 PM 4. Patience is a cornerstone of life.	**17** ♅⚷♇♆℞ ▲ ☽→♑ 4:07 AM 5. Relax with a variety of options.	**18** ♅⚷♇♆℞ ▲ 6. Eat healthy food.	**19** ♅⚷♇♆℞ Yom Kippur ☽-V/C 10:09 AM ☽→♒ 4:51 PM 7. Learn what is best to prosper.	**20** ♅⚷♇♆℞ 8. Generosity increases your wealth.	**21** ♅⚷♇♆℞ ☽-V/C 10:13 AM ☿→♎ 8:41 PM 9. Pray for others well-being.	**22** ♅⚷♇♆℞ Autumn Equinox ☽→♓ 5:26 AM ☉→♎ 6:55 PM 10. Today creates tomorrow.
23 ♅⚷♇♆℞ ☽-V/C 10:25 PM 11. Stay universally connected.	**24** ♅⚷♇♆℞ ☽→♈ 4:03 PM ○ 1°♈59′ - 7:52 PM 3. Kindness goes a long way.	**25** ♅⚷♇♆℞ ⚷℞→♓ - 5:12 PM 4. Maybe you need to follow the directions.	**26** ♅⚷♇♆℞ ☽-V/C 3:28 AM 5. Make changes with ease and grace.	**27** ♅⚷♇♆℞ ☽→♉ 12:15 AM 6. Try a new recipe for dinner.	**28** ♅⚷♇♆℞ ☽-V/C 3:36 PM 7. Let your smarts pay off.	**29** ♅⚷♇♆℞ ☽→♊ 6:25 AM 8. People thrive with a dependable leader.
30 ♅⚷♆℞ ☽-V/C 8:37 AM ♇SD - 18°♑45′ - 8:31 PM 9. Where can you volunteer to help?						

♈ Aries	♍ Virgo	♓ Pisces	♃ Jupiter	➡ Enters	2. Balance	8. Money
♉ Taurus	♎ Libra	☉ Sun	♄ Saturn	℞ Retrograde	3. Fun	9. Spirituality
♊ Gemini	♏ Scorpio	☽ Moon	♅ Uranus	SD Stationary Direct	4. Structure	10. Visionary
♋ Cancer	♐ Sagittarius	☿ Mercury	♆ Neptune	V/C Void-of-Course	5. Action	11. Completion
♌ Leo	♑ Capricorn	♀ Venus	♇ Pluto	▲ Super Sensitivity	6. Love	
	♒ Aquarius	♂ Mars	⚷ Chiron	▼ Low Vitality	7. Learning	

New Moon in Virgo

When the Sun is in Virgo

Virgo is called the "Womb of Time" in which the seeds of great value are planted, shielded, nourished, and revealed. It is the labor of Virgo that brings the Christ Principle into manifestation within individuals and humanity. This unification occurs when we feel the power within us to serve. When we serve, we give birth to Divinity. Virgo time is when we all have a chance to raise the standard of excellence in our lives and on the Earth. The Virgo intelligence stores and maintains light in a precise manner. Attention to detail is Virgo's great gift to life.

Virgo Goddess

Mayan Goddess of medicine and midwifery, Ixchel, enters quietly in her jaguar form, to sit and observe. How are you being healed and how are you assisting the healing of others? Jaguar medicine is powerful for clearing attachments and cords that no longer serve you.

Call upon Ixchel to help you find precision and clarity through your words. Let her help you end negative self-talk. Enlist her to walk your boundaries and protect you fiercely, as though you were her little cub. Locate a stone or amulet you can carry in your pocket to remind you of her power, just like shaman and physicians of old would carry in their medicine bundles. When Ixchel has your back, you can roar!

Build Your Altar

Colors	Earth tones, blue, green
Numerology	6 – Live love every day
Tarot Card	The Hermit – Being a shining light for all of life
Gemstones	Emerald, malachite, sapphire
Plant Remedy	Sagebrush – The ability to hold and store light
Fragrance	Lavender – Management and storage of energy

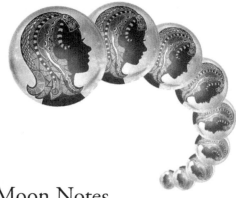

Moon Notes

September 9th, 11:01 AM

New Moon 17° Virgo 0'
New moons are about manifestation, planting seeds, and becoming fruitful.

Statement	I Heal
Body	Intestines
Mind	Critical
Spirit	Divinity in the details

Element
Earth – Practical, determined, structured, enduring, stubborn, traditional, stable, and stuck inside the box.

Choice Points
Light	Mental exploration
Shadow	Superstitious fear
Wisdom	Contribute by sparking new life into dull or apathetic situations.

Sabian Symbol
Two girls playing with a Ouija board.

Potential
Curiosity leads to messages and inner guidance.

10th House Moon I Produce/I Heal

Umbrella Energy
Your approach to status, career, honor, and prestige, and why you chose your Father.

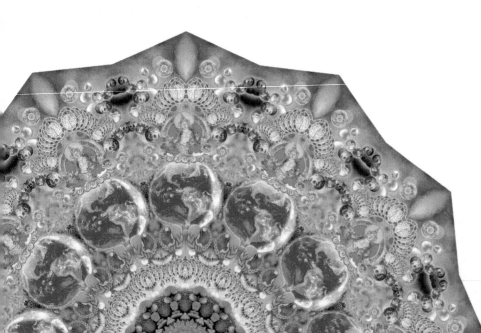

Virgo Victories & Challenges

Say all of the statements in this section out loud. Then, underline the phrase that means the most to you. Use the phrase as your affirmation for recalibrating throughout this moon phase.

Today, I recognize what I love most about myself. I am the source of my love, my life, and my experience. I will set aside time today to nurture myself. I allow myself to receive these gifts and know in my heart that it is natural for me to love myself. I discover, deep within myself, the knowing that the love I give myself is commensurate to the love I am willing to receive from others. I am aware that what I expect from others cannot be truly expressed or experienced if I cannot give to myself first. I can never be disappointed when I know that love is a natural resource for me today.

Today, I honor the Earth by acknowledging what she has given me. I take time out to walk in the woods or on the beach, to feel the power of the creative pulse of the creative forces flowing through my body with the energy of being alive. I spend time in my garden and plant flowers to enhance the idea of beauty today. I honor my body today and get a massage. I spend quality time sharing joyful moments with those who love to connect from the heart and realize the blessings that come from living my life with love.

Virgo Homework

Virgos manifest best through working with herbology, folk medicine, environmental industries, organic farming, recycling, horticulture, acupuncture, healing arts, nutritional counseling, yoga instruction, and editing.

The Virgo moon cycle gives birth to Divinity in its own unique way, understanding the Soul's blueprint to be a temple of beauty. This creates what is known as the "crisis of perfection" within the minds of humankind during this time. We become aware of Spirit ascending and descending at the same time and must recognize that these contradicting energies are working within us in order to give birth to Divinity.

Victory List

Acknowledge what you have overcome.
Keep this list active during this moon cycle.
Honoring victory allows you to accept success.

Sky Power Yoga

Seated Spinal Twist

You need one chair
for the prop.

With your back straight sit one hand-width from the back of the chair with your feet on the floor hip-width apart. If your feet require more solid contact with the floor, place pillows or folded towels under your feet.

Reach your right hand back to hold the chair just behind your sitting bones. Reach your left hand diagonally to cup the right knee.

While gazing forward, anchor your sitting bones into the chair. Then inhale and lengthen your spine.

Relax. Close your eyes. Breathe in and out slowly and deeply several times through your nose with your awareness on your intestines.

Inhale deeply as you say or think to yourself the mantra *I Heal*.

As you exhale softly, twist to turn your head towards your right shoulder using a subtle, gentle rotation. Feel your breath expanding your rib cage on the left side as well as massaging the spine and internal organs.

After several breaths, gently release the pose, return to facing forward, and repeat on the opposite side.

172

Manifesting List

Virgo Manifesting Ideas

Now is the time to focus on manifesting a high standard of excellence, a healthy lifestyle, self-acceptance, discernment without judgment, healing abilities, a contribution to nature, and a healthy body.

This or something better than this comes to me in an easy and pleasurable way, for the good of all concerned. Thank you, Universe!

New Moon in Virgo

Your Personal Moon Experience

Fill in the Cosmic Check-In page. Then look up the degree of the Moon on the chart below. Take note of the "I" statement on the outside of the wheel where the Moon is located. Now, locate the same degree on your own chart and make a note of the house and corresponding "I" statement. Go back to the Cosmic Check-In page and circle the two statements from the charts and read what you wrote. This will give you an idea about what to expect from this moon phase on a personal level. For more information on personalizing your *Moon Book*, go to www.BlueMoonAcademy.com and look for *How to Use the Moon Book*.

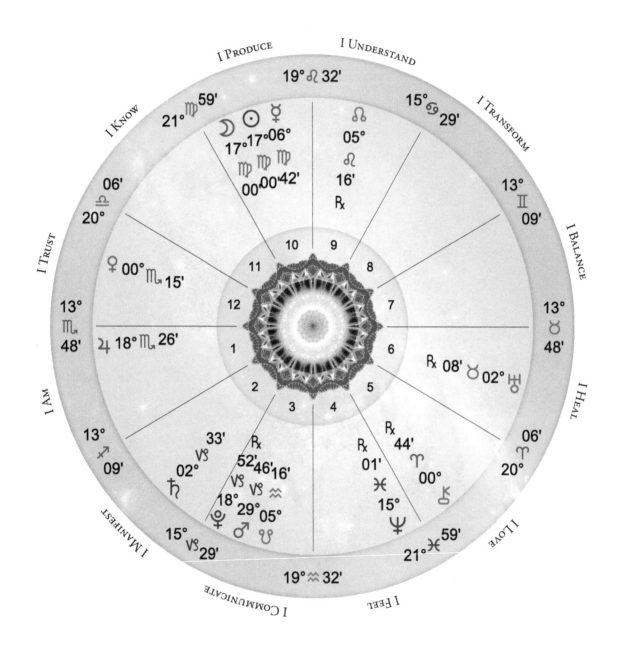

♈	Aries	♋	Cancer	♏	Scorpio	♓	Pisces	♀	Venus	♅	Uranus	☊	North Node
♉	Taurus	♌	Leo	♐	Sagittarius	☉	Sun	♂	Mars	♆	Neptune	☋	South Node
♊	Gemini	♍	Virgo	♑	Capricorn	☽	Moon	♃	Jupiter	♇	Pluto	℞	Retrograde
		♎	Libra	♒	Aquarius	☿	Mercury	♄	Saturn	⚷	Chiron		

Cosmic Check-in

Virgo New Moon
September 9th
11:01 AM

Take a moment to write a brief phrase for each "I" statement.
This activates all areas of your life for this creative cycle.

♍ I Heal

♎ I Balance

♏ I Transform

♐ I Understand

♑ I Produce

♒ I Know

♓ I Trust

♈ I Am

♉ I Manifest

♊ I Communicate

♋ I Feel

♌ I Love

Full Moon in Aries

When the Sun is Opposite the Moon

Full moons are always in opposition to the Sun. This creates a feeling of tension between where you want to shine and how your feelings are flowing on a sensory level about the Sun's directive. The two forces seem like they are working against each other, yet they are on the same team displaying different techniques to obtain the same mission. The Aries/Libra polarity creates tension between "I Am" and "We Are".

Aries Goddess

Heqet, the Fertility Goddess of the early dynastic period of Egypt, is often depicted on the amulets of pregnant women as a frog sitting on a lotus. Associated with germination of corn following the flooding of the Nile (when frogs were most prolific), and with the final stages of childbirth, she is said to breathe the "breath of life" into the bodies of newborn children who are formed on the potter's wheel of her partner Khnum. It was she who breathed life into Horus, in the myth of Isis and Osiris.

The moonlight is now shining on you as you take your self-confidence and self-awareness to a new level. Is it time for you to take on a new role within your community? Have you developed new knowledge, skills, and qualities that you're ready to try out? Ask Heqet to assist you through the stages from tadpole to adult, as you lose your tail and develop your sea legs.

Build Your Altar

Colors	Red, black, coral
Numerology	3 – Kindness goes a long way
Tarot Card	Tower – Release from a stuck place, a major breakthrough
Gemstones	Diamond, red jasper, coral, obsidian
Plant remedy	Oak, pomegranate – Planting new life and rooting new life
Fragrance	Ginger – The ability to ingest and digest life

Moon Notes

September 24th, 7:52 PM

Full Moon 1° Aries 59'
Full Moons are about releasing, letting go, becoming free, and recalibrating.

Statement	I Am
Body	Head and face
Mind	Ego
Spirit	Awakening

Element
Fire – Igniting, dissolving, accelerating, cleansing, advancing awareness, impatience, leadership, passion, and vitality.

Choice Points
Light	Objective awareness
Shadow	Evasive
Wisdom	It's time to manifest an idea, make it real.

Sabian Symbol
A comedian reveals human nature.

Potential
Being silly is a good way to gain acceptance.

12th House Moon I Trust/I Am

Umbrella Energy
Determines how you deal with your karma, unconscious software, and what you will experience in order to attain mastery by completing your karma. It is also about the way you connect to the Divine.

Karmic Awakening
Scorpio/Taurus – Your money or my money?

Clearing the Slate

Sixty hours before the full moon negative traits connected to the astro-sign might become activated to trigger what needs to be released during the full moon phase. You may notice a sudden need to be first or impatience that could lead to anger or arrogance. Make a list, look in the mirror, and for each negative trait, tell yourself *I am sorry, I forgive you, thank you for your awareness,* and *I love you.*

Aries Victories & Challenges

Say all of the statements in this section out loud. Then, underline the phrase that means the most to you. Use the phrase as your affirmation for recalibrating throughout this moon phase.

Today, I let go. I trust that whatever breaks down or breaks through is a blessing in disguise for me. I make a commitment to allow myself to be spontaneous and live in the moment. I know the unexpected is a blessing for me and a way for me to make a breakthrough out of my limitations. I am aware that I am resistant to change. I know I must make changes and am too stubborn to take the appropriate action myself to change. I have built many walls of false protection around me, guarding me and blocking me from the reality that change is a constant. I have freeze-framed my life and desire support to update myself. I have allowed my fear of change to become my false motto and my life is at a standstill. I am unwilling to use any more energy to perpetuate my resistance. I know that continuing to cling to the past is a waste of my energy. I can no longer put things off that delay my process. I feel the breaking down of form. I trust that all changes are in my favor. All changes lead me to golden opportunities. I release false pride. I release false foundations. I release false authorities. In so doing, I allow for everything to crumble around me so I can see that my true strength is within and I will build my life from the inside out.

I am ready for new experiences. I am ready for the unexpected. I am willing to have an event occur so I can become activated towards my breakthrough. I am ready for the power of now. I know being spontaneous will bring me to true joy. I know if I ride this carrier wave it will take me to a place far beyond my scope of limited thinking. I know the will of God works in my favor and knows more than I do in any given moment.

Aries Homework

Now you are ready to take a personal inventory on behaviors such as impatience, talking over people, brat attacks, and starting every sentence with "I."

This is a time when the light becomes a prisoner of polarized forces. This diminishing light begins its yearly sojourn beneath the surface, asking us to balance light and dark by mastering the concept of equilibrium. Equilibrium is the Law of Harmony, where we attempt to reach a state of achievement by combining paradoxical fields that break the crystallization of polarity. Spend time looking for increasing and decreasing fields of light around you.

Gratitude List

Keep this list active throughout the moon cycle. This will bring you to a level of completion so that a new cycle of opportunity can occur in your life. Be prepared for miracles!

Sky Power Yoga

Resting Pose

You need one pillow and one blanket for the prop.

Lie on your back with your legs spread shoulder-width apart. Place your arms by your side at a 45-degree angle with your palms facing down. You may place a pillow under your neck for support or cover yourself with a blanket to stay warm.

Relax. Close your eyes. Breathe in and

out slowly and deeply several times through your nose with your awareness on your head. Allow your body to soften and relax until it feels like you are melting into the floor.

Feel the gentle rhythmic massage of the body as your belly subtly rises and falls with each breath. Allow this awareness to increase your sense of being grounded and supported.

Inhale and envision the energy of your breath coming up from the earth into your feet and then up your legs, your spine, and out the top of your head. Say or think to yourself the mantra *I Am*.

Exhale softly and slowly as you envision your breath flowing back into your head and down your spine, your legs, and out your feet back into the earth. Repeat as desired.

Freedom List

Say this statement out loud three times before writing your list:

I am a free spiritual being and it is my desire to be free to think and to express myself fully.

Aries
Recalibrating Ideas

Now is the time to activate a game change in my life, and give up anger as a default, competition and comparison, irritation and struggle, the need to be first, overdoing it and not resting, impatience, impulsiveness, and hostility.

From this day forward I resolve to be true – first to myself and my highest self, and then to the highest self in me which is the Source of Love That I Am.

181

Full Moon in Aries

Your Personal Moon Experience

Fill in the Cosmic Check-In page. Then look up the degree of the Moon on the chart below. Take note of the "I" statement on the outside of the wheel where the Moon is located. Now, locate the same degree on your own chart and make a note of the house and corresponding "I" statement. Go back to the Cosmic Check-In page, circle the two statements from the charts, and read what you wrote. This will give you an idea about what to expect from this moon phase on a personal level. For a personalized *My Moon Experience* Astrology reading with Beatrex, go to www.beatrex.com.

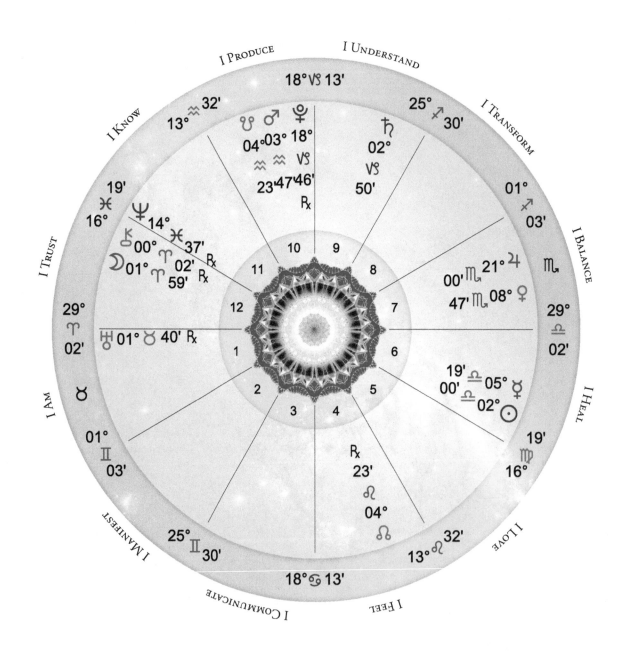

♈ Aries	♋ Cancer	♏ Scorpio	♓ Pisces	♀ Venus	♅ Uranus	☊ North Node
♉ Taurus	♌ Leo	♐ Sagittarius	☉ Sun	♂ Mars	♆ Neptune	☋ South Node
♊ Gemini	♍ Virgo	♑ Capricorn	☿ Mercury	♃ Jupiter	♇ Pluto	℞ Retrograde
	♎ Libra	♒ Aquarius	☽ Moon	♄ Saturn	⚷ Chiron	

Cosmic Check-in

Aries Full Moon
September 24th
7:52 PM

Take a moment to write a brief phrase for each "I" statement.
This activates all areas of your life for this creative cycle.

♈ I Am

♉ I Manifest

♊ I Communicate

♋ I Feel

♌ I Love

♍ I Heal

♎ I Balance

♏ I Transform

♐ I Understand

♑ I Produce

♒ I Know

♓ I Trust

October

Jupiter in Scorpio squares Pluto in Capricorn until 2019

Expect major transformation to be graceful and beneficial. Be open and all will be well.

October 1-2, 28-29: Low Vitality

We need to monitor our energy to avoid burnout.

October 5: Venus retrograde in Scorpio

Expect old lovers to show up. Be open so you can clear up any old news and be clear that hidden agendas may keep you from your highest and best outcomes.

October 8-15: Venus in Scorpio opposite Uranus in Taurus

Do your best to keep things above the surface. Perhaps you think it is best to leave the wool over others' eyes. Not a good idea when Uranus is involved. Expect for hidden ideas or forces to blow out of the water. Truth is the answer here. You may also find yourself taking back impulse shopping items to the store.

October 8: Venus retrograde conjunct Jupiter in Scorpio

Expect to go deep on all levels especially where relating is concerned. Let it all hang out and know that blessings will take place.

October 9: Mercury enters Scorpio

Time to share your deepest secrets and trust that they will be kept sacred. What is said or experienced in Scorpio stays in Scorpio.

October 14-15: Super Sensitivity

Expect chaos and avoid it, and all will be well.

October 23: Sun enters Scorpio

We enter into darkness during this time and whatever you can't deal with gets placed in the shadow to be dealt with at a later date.

October 24: Venus retrograde conjunct Sun in Scorpio

Accept the power from your past and see if it wishes to recalibrate into 'the now' and become present to a more powerful perspective.

October 24: Moon and Uranus coupled in Scorpio

This is a very explosive pattern for women, especially for mother/daughter relationships.

October 24: Jupiter and Mercury coupled in Scorpio

Speak from your heart and rewards will come your way.

October 30: Mercury enters Sagittarius

Travel far and near, big trips and small trips… the 'adventure button' has been pressed. Go for it!

October 31: Venus retrograde backs into Libra

This is a good time for reworking any unfinished business where relationships and partnerships are concerned. Shine lights on your regrets and release resentments.

Sunday	Monday	Tuesday	Wednesday	Thursday	Friday	Saturday
	1 ♅⚷♆℞ ▼ ☽→♋ 11:00 AM 10. A new vision sets you free.	**2** ♅⚷♆℞ ▼ 11. Feel the vastness of the Universe.	**3** ♅⚷♆℞ ☽-V/C 1:33 AM ☽→♌ 2:12 PM 3. Put on your party shoes and dance.	**4** ♅⚷♆℞ 4. Make a logical plan.	**5** ♀♅⚷♆℞ ☽-V/C 4:33 AM ☽→♍ 4:19 PM ♀ S/R 10°♏50' - 12:06 PM 5. Plan an outdoor adventure.	**6** ♀♅⚷♆℞ 6. Expect romance to be in the air.
7 ♀♅⚷♆℞ ☽-V/C 7:02 AM ☽→♎ 6:10 PM 7. Enjoy the depth of your mind.	**8** ♀♅⚷♆℞ Columbus Day ● 15°♎48' - 8:46 PM 8. Admit that you love money.	**9** ♀♅⚷♆℞ ☽-V/C 1:50 AM ☽→♏ 9:09 PM ☿→♏ 5:41 PM 9. Be of service to the earth.	**10** ♀♅⚷♆℞ 10. Let your dreams come true.	**11** ♀♅⚷♆℞ ☽-V/C 4:12 PM 11. Every thing counts.	**12** ♀♅⚷♆℞ ☽→♐ 2:52 AM 3. Be juicy and go shopping.	**13** ♀♅⚷♆℞ ☽-V/C 5:58 PM 4. Team spirit makes winners.
14 ♀♅⚷♆℞ ▲ ☽→♑ 12:16 PM 5. Change brings benefits.	**15** ♀♅⚷♆℞ ▲ 6. Relax with music and candles.	**16** ♀♅⚷♆℞ ☽-V/C 2:49 PM 7. Think big.	**17** ♀♅⚷♆℞ ☽→♒ 12:35 AM 8. Manifest your heart's desire.	**18** ♀♅⚷♆℞ 9. Your audience awaits you.	**19** ♀♅⚷♆℞ ☽-V/C 5:27 AM ☽→♓ 1:20 PM 10. Celebrate what's new and good.	**20** ♀♅⚷♆℞ 3. Take your kids to Disneyland.
21 ♀♅⚷♆℞ ☽-V/C 4:47 PM ☽→♈ 11:58 PM 4. Know your boundaries.	**22** ♀♅⚷♆℞ 5. Remove unconscious limitations.	**23** ♀♅⚷♆℞ ☽-V/C 11:17 AM ☉→♏ 4:24 AM 6. Bring new colors into your life.	**24** ♀♅⚷♆℞ ☽→♉ 7:33 AM ○ 1°♉13' - 9:45AM 7. Take on a research project.	**25** ♀♅⚷♆℞ 8. Buy a lottery ticket.	**26** ♀♅⚷♆℞ ☽-V/C 7:48 AM ☽→♊ 12:40 PM 9. Trust your heart to show you the way.	**27** ♀♅⚷♆℞ ☽-V/C 9:37 PM 10. Be open to new technology.
28 ♀♅⚷♆℞ ▼ ☽→♋ 4:27 PM 11. Let the Universe guide you.	**29** ♀♅⚷♆℞ ▼ 3. Dance the night away.	**30** ♀♅⚷♆℞ ☽-V/C 7:30 PM ☽→♌ 7:41 PM ☿→♐ 9:39 PM 4. Organize your filing system.	**31** ♀♅⚷♆℞ Halloween ♀→♎ 12:43 PM 5. Let your costume change your reality.			

♈ Aries	♍ Virgo	♓ Pisces	♃ Jupiter	→ Enters	2. Balance	8. Money
♉ Taurus	♎ Libra	☉ Sun	♄ Saturn	℞ Retrograde	3. Fun	9. Spirituality
♊ Gemini	♏ Scorpio	☽ Moon	♅ Uranus	S/D Stationary Direct	4. Structure	10. Visionary
♋ Cancer	♐ Sagittarius	☿ Mercury	♆ Neptune	V/C Void-of-Course	5. Action	11. Completion
♌ Leo	♑ Capricorn	♀ Venus	♇ Pluto	▲ Super Sensitivity	6. Love	
	♒ Aquarius	♂ Mars	⚷ Chiron	▼ Low Vitality	7. Learning	

New Moon in Libra

When the Sun is in Libra

Libra energy gives us the opportunity to bridge the gap between the higher and lower mind; abstract thinking versus concrete thinking. During Libra time, the light and dark forces are in balance and you are given a chance to experience harmony. Harmony occurs when you keep your polarities in motion and put paradox to rest, thus breaking the crystallization of polarity. Now is the time to weigh your values through the light of your Soul. Libra asks you to look at what is increasing and decreasing in your life. Start with friendship, courage, sincerity, and understanding, and keep going until your scale is in motion.

Libra Goddess

The Black Madonna, is a goddess archetype found all over the world, in her many associations as Isis, Mary Magdalene, Sara, Kali, or Virgin of Guadalupe. She offers up compassion and understanding for the human condition. Black is all colors, completely absorbed, and in her blackness she encompasses all and gives solace and miracles to any seeking comfort. Often depicted with a child in arms, a halo or ring of stars around her head, and a moon at her feet, the Black Madonna is the protectress of those who are marginalized. She is connected seamlessly to Heaven and Earth, as a fully incarnated woman and mother who has known deep sorrow, passion, joy, and love.

Grant her real life experience equal weight with the images of virginal perfection offered up as ideal, and she will help you have compassion for yourself and others experiencing the struggle of living and relating.

Build Your Altar

Colors	Pink, green
Numerology	8 – Admit that you love money
Tarot Card	Justice – The Law of Cause and Effect
Gemstones	Jade, rose quartz
Plant Remedy	Olive trees – Stamina
Fragrance	Eucalyptus – Clarity of breath

Moon Notes

October 8th, 8:46 PM

New Moon 15° Libra 48'
New moons are about manifestation, planting seeds, and becoming fruitful.

Statement	I Balance
Body	Kidneys
Mind	Social
Spirit	Peace

Element
Air – The breath of life that allows the mind to achieve new insights and fresh perspectives, inspiration, active and abstract dreaming, and freedom from attachments.

Choice Points
Light	Positive attitude
Shadow	Inertia
Wisdom	Your process for the Earth, release what you process.

Sabian Symbol
After a storm a boat landing stands in need of reconstruction.

Potential
Create a plan of action so life can move on.

5th House Moon I Love/I Balance

Umbrella Energy
The way you love and how you want to be loved.

Karmic Awakening
Scorpio/Taurus – Your money or my money?

Libra Victories & Challenges

Say all of the statements in this section out loud. Then, underline the phrase that means the most to you. Use the phrase as your affirmation for recalibrating throughout this moon phase.

I feel the call of the higher worlds awakening me to a new vibration. This call is to move beyond judgment and move to a place of acceptance, understanding, unconditional confidence, and love. I am at a place in my life where I can embrace the world of acceptance and wholeness, because I have birthed myself anew, beyond the imprisonment and crystallization of polarity and righteousness. My black and white worlds of right and wrong have integrated and blended into gray, the color of wisdom, where true knowledge exists. Knowledge simply is, and the need for proof does not exist where wisdom lives.

The only requirement is experience. I know that everything that comes before me is a direct reflection of my own experience and, in embracing this concept, I can now receive the gift of infinite awareness. I am in a place of awareness that came before and goes beyond where good and evil exist. I have within me, the presence of unconditional confidence to go where true love lives. I no longer need to prove myself. I am now simply being myself. I release the need to be right and accept the right to BE. I no longer need to be forgiven, because I am neither wrong nor right. I no longer need to define myself. Acceptance has no reason for defense. I no longer need to be guilty; duty motivation is no longer a reality. I know that where there is judgment, there is separation. I know understanding unifies. I accept the call of the higher worlds and express myself freely and fully without fear of judgment. I accept myself as I am, so I can learn what I can become.

Libra Homework

Libras manifest best through the legal industry, beauty industry, diplomatic service, match-making, urban development, mediation, feng shui, spa ownership, clutter-busting and space clearing, romance writing, wedding consulting, fashion design, and as librarians.

It is time to weigh and measure the values of relationship, friendship, courage, sensitivity, sincerity, and understanding. Look at what is increasing and what is decreasing in these areas.

Victory List

Acknowledge what you have overcome.
Keep this list active during this moon cycle.
Honoring victory allows you to accept success.

Sky Power Yoga

Seated Forward Fold

You need one chair for the prop.

With your back straight sit one hand-width from the back of the chair with your feet on the floor hip-width apart. If your feet require more solid contact with the floor, place pillows or folded towels under your feet.

Place hands on thighs just above knees. While gazing forward, anchor your sitting bones into the chair. Then inhale and lengthen your spine and neck towards the ceiling.

Relax. Close your eyes. Breathe in and out slowly and deeply several times through your nose with your awareness on your kidneys.

Inhale softly as you say or think to yourself the mantra *I Balance*. Exhale slowly, hinging at the hips with a straight back (hands slide forward over knees and down shins towards the floor). Stop once you feel any tightness in the back of your legs.

Release the neck and drop your head slightly. Inhale and exhale in this position for a few breaths.

Bring your head back to neutral in line with the spine, engage your abdominals, straighten your spine and return to sitting upright facing forward. Repeat as desired.

Manifesting List

Libra
Manifesting Ideas

Now is the time to focus on manifesting relationships, wholeness, being loving, lovable, and loved, living life as an art form, balance and equality, integrity, accuracy, diplomacy, and peace.

This or something better than this comes to me in an easy and pleasurable way, for the good of all concerned. Thank you, Universe!

New Moon in Libra

Your Personal Moon Experience

Fill in the Cosmic Check-In page. Then look up the degree of the Moon on the chart below. Take note of the "I" statement on the outside of the wheel where the Moon is located. Now, locate the same degree on your own chart and make a note of the house and corresponding "I" statement. Go back to the Cosmic Check-In page and circle the two statements from the charts and read what you wrote. This will give you an idea about what to expect from this moon phase on a personal level. For more information on personalizing your *Moon Book*, go to www.BlueMoonAcademy.com and look for *How to Use the Moon Book*.

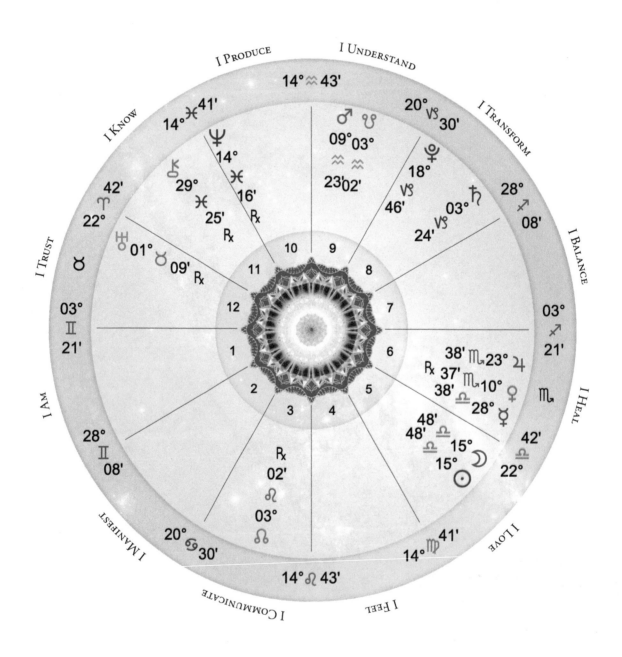

	Aries		Cancer		Scorpio		Pisces		Venus		Uranus		North Node
	Taurus		Leo		Sagittarius		Sun		Mars		Neptune		South Node
	Gemini		Virgo		Capricorn		Moon		Jupiter		Pluto		Retrograde
			Libra		Aquarius		Mercury		Saturn		Chiron		

Cosmic Check-in

Libra New Moon
October 8th
8:46 PM

Take a moment to write a brief phrase for each "I" statement.
This activates all areas of your life for this creative cycle.

♎ I Balance

♏ I Transform

♐ I Understand

♑ I Produce

♒ I Know

♓ I Trust

♈ I Am

♉ I Manifest

♊ I Communicate

♋ I Feel

♌ I Love

♍ I Heal

Full Moon in Taurus

When the Sun is Opposite the Moon

Full moons are always in opposition to the Sun. This creates a feeling of tension between where you want to shine and how your feelings are flowing on a sensory level about the Sun's directive. The two forces seem like they are working against each other, yet they are on the same team displaying different techniques to obtain the same mission. The Taurus/Scorpio polarity creates tension between "my" money and "our" money.

Taurus Goddess

The Roman Goddess of Abundance and Opportunity, Copia, invites you to drink deeply from her overflowing horn of plenty. As you harvest the bounties of your desires from the seeds you planted last Spring, thank Copia for the increase in your abundance factor! There is no greater prayer than the act of giving thanks.

During this Taurus moon, let receptivity and gratitude be in your attitude and actions! With open hands and heart, ask for Copia's presence at your table, and allow her to fill your cup with blessings. Encourage your gratitude to expand and generously influence all with whom you interact.

Build Your Altar

Colors	Scarlet, earth tones
Numerology	7 – Take on a research project
Tarot Card	Hierophant – Spiritual authority
Gemstones	Red coral, red agate, garnet
Plant remedy	Angelica – Connecting Heaven and Earth
Fragrance	Rose – Opening the heart

Moon Notes

October 24th, 9:45 AM

Full Moon 1° Taurus 13'
  Full Moons are about releasing, letting go, becoming free, and recalibrating.

Statement I Manifest

Body Neck

Mind Collector

Spirit Accumulation

Element
  Earth – Practical, determined, structured, enduring, stubborn, traditional, stable, and stuck inside the box.

Choice Points
Light	Awe-inspiring
Shadow	Dread
Wisdom	Find new healing techniques for your body.

Sabian Symbol
  An electrical storm.

Potential
  A new light advances heaven and earth.

5th House Moon I Love/I Manifest

Umbrella Energy
  The way you love and how you want to be loved.

Clearing the Slate

Sixty hours before the full moon negative traits connected to the astro-sign might become activated to trigger what needs to be released during the full moon phase. You may notice a sudden unwillingness to share or find yourself being stubborn, wasteful, or resisting change. Make a list, look in the mirror, and for each negative trait, tell yourself *I am sorry, I forgive you, thank you for your awareness,* and *I love you.*

Taurus Victories & Challenges

Say all of the statements in this section out loud. Then, under-line the phrase that means the most to you. Use the phrase as your affirmation for recalibrating throughout this moon phase.

Everything is possible for me today. My possibilities are endless. I have the power within me to make all of my dreams come true. I have the tools to make my talent a reality. I have the power to identify with my talent. Today, I focus my attention and intention on manifesting with my talent and, in so doing, I transform my ideas into reality. I recognize the part of me that is connected to the cosmic source of ideas and I express that source within me to manifest my creative power. I see my possibilities and act on them today. I am the creative power. I am all-knowing. I am an individual. There is no one else like me. I can manifest anything I desire. I intend it, I allow it, so be it.

Rules for Manifesting

Know what you want. Write it down. Say it out loud. Recognize that because you thought it, it can be so. Release your limiting beliefs. Override your limiting beliefs with power statements. Act as if you have already manifested your idea. Lastly, value yourself!

Taurus Homework

Taureans manifest best when buying, selling, and owning real estate, gardening and landscaping, selling and collecting art, manufacturing and selling fine furniture, singing or acting, and as a restaurateur, antique dealer, or interior designer.

The Taurus moon asks us to infuse light into form and, in so doing, the bridge between humanity and divinity is actualized and we can assume our stewardship in the physical world. When we release Spirit into matter, we become open to the idea that accumulation and actualization set us free to experience the abundance available to us here on Earth. Go shopping!

Gratitude List

Keep this list active throughout the moon cycle. This will bring you to a level of completion so that a new cycle of opportunity can occur in your life. Be prepared for miracles!

Sky Power Yoga

Seated Fish

You need one chair for the prop.

With your back straight sit one hand-width from the back of the chair with your feet on the floor hip-width apart. If your feet require more solid contact with the floor, place pillows or folded towels under your feet.

Place hands on the sides of the chair with elbows pulled in slightly and pointing towards the chair back.

Gently lift your chest from the sternum with your head and neck remaining neutral.

Relax. Close your eyes. Breathe in and out slowly and deeply several times through your nose with your awareness on your neck.

Inhale softly as you say or think to yourself the mantra *I Manifest*. Tilt the chin upward slightly as you envision the energy of mantra in your throat. Remain for three breaths.

On the next exhale, softly and slowly release the chin and the elbows. Ground your breath and the mantra into the earth as you release the pose. Repeat as desired.

Freedom List

Say this statement out loud three times before writing your list:

I am a free spiritual being and it is my desire to be free to think and to express myself fully.

Taurus
Recalibrating Ideas

Now is the time to activate a game change in my life, and give up envy, financial insecurity, being stubborn, hoarding, addictive spending, not feeling valuable, and fear of change.

From this day forward I resolve to be true — first to myself and my highest self, and then to the highest self in me which is the Source of Love That I Am.

Full Moon in Taurus

Your Personal Moon Experience

Fill in the Cosmic Check-In page. Then look up the degree of the Moon on the chart below. Take note of the "I" statement on the outside of the wheel where the Moon is located. Now, locate the same degree on your own chart and make a note of the house and corresponding "I" statement. Go back to the Cosmic Check-In page, circle the two statements from the charts, and read what you wrote. This will give you an idea about what to expect from this moon phase on a personal level. For a personalized *My Moon Experience* Astrology reading with Beatrex, go to www.beatrex.com.

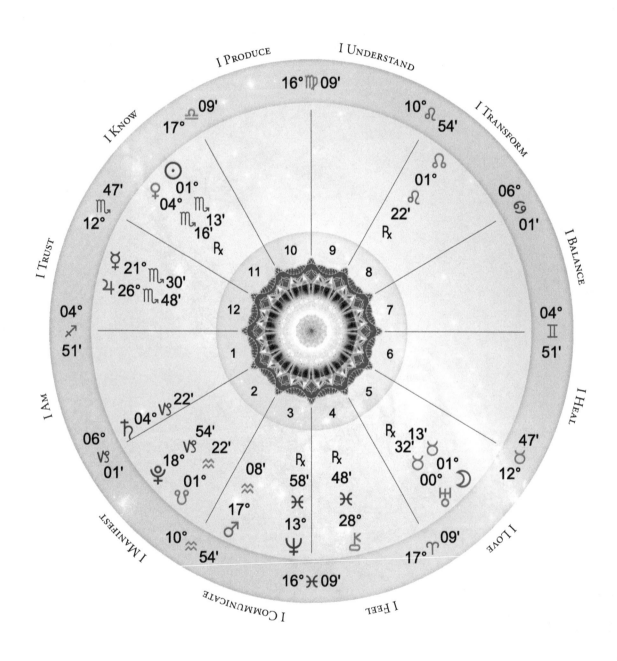

♈	Aries	♋	Cancer	♏	Scorpio	♓	Pisces	♀	Venus	♅	Uranus	☊	North Node
♉	Taurus	♌	Leo	♐	Sagittarius	☉	Sun	♂	Mars	♆	Neptune	☋	South Node
♊	Gemini	♍	Virgo	♑	Capricorn	☽	Moon	♃	Jupiter	♇	Pluto	℞	Retrograde
		♎	Libra	♒	Aquarius	☿	Mercury	♄	Saturn	⚷	Chiron		

Cosmic Check-in

Taurus Full Moon
October 24th
9:45 AM

Take a moment to write a brief phrase for each "I" statement.
This activates all areas of your life for this creative cycle.

♉ I Manifest

♊ I Communicate

♋ I Feel

♌ I Love

♍ I Heal

♎ I Balance

♏ I Transform

♐ I Understand

♑ I Produce

♒ I Know

♓ I Trust

♈ I Am

November

November 6: Uranus retrograde backs into Aries

A reminder not to forget the teachings of the last few years about the power of presence. Remember your "I Am" statements will tell you about accepting your personal power. Your personal power is your ticket to your position in the future. The future becomes very important today especially for the United States.

November 6: North Node enters Cancer

The future focus, direction, and intention of the United States becomes very evident and alignment will come into being for the good of all concerned. Pay attention to the climate of your feelings and the feelings around you, it will be a telltale sign.

November 7: Uranus retrograde in Aries opposite Venus retrograde in Libra

Polarity is at work here. Notice where you feel pulled away from your priority of self development and where you turn your attention away from self in order to make someone else happy. The 'brat attacks' are part of this equation and could get noisy if lack of attention is happening.

November 7: Pluto conjunct South Node retrograde in Capricorn opposite North Node retrograde in Cancer

The South Node retrograde dancing with Pluto is a telltale sign that something has to give. Recalibration is totally necessary so evolution can happen. The South Node demands that the process must end. It is already obsolete and no longer fashionable to hold on. The North Node puts our future in focus and it is in our best interest to go for it.

November 8: Jupiter enters Sagittarius

Just in time for the holidays, this is wondrous! Feel the fun returning, the adventure, and the advancement of knowledge.

November 9-11: Super Sensitivity

Do what you can to avoid the chaos and all will be well.

November 15: Mars enters Pisces

Yikes! Expect a steam cleaning of your feelings to happen. Express yourself.

November 16: Venus retrograde in Libra

Relationships are up for review. Instead of griping and complaining, go beneath the triggers and express your truth. Remember when speaking to follow Buddha's teaching and ask before speaking, "Is it kind?" "Is it truthful?" "Is it necessary?"

November 16: Mercury retrograde in Sagittarius

'Foot-in-mouth disease' could happen often. If you are thick-skinned you will be fine, if not, get your hankie out and be prepared to sniffle.

November 22: Sun enters Sagittarius

Brightness returns to the planet, prepare to celebrate.

November 24: Neptune goes direct in Pisces

Your Spiritual pathway becomes clear. Get a pedicure to cleanse your feet, then start walking on it. Better results will happen for you with clean feet.

November 24-25: Low Vitality

Earth changes are possible so stay close to home.

SUNDAY	MONDAY	TUESDAY	WEDNESDAY	THURSDAY	FRIDAY	SATURDAY
				1 ♀♅⚷♆℞ ☽-V/C 9:31 PM ☽→♍ 10:47 PM 6. Revitalize by bringing in flowers.	**2** ♀♅⚷♆℞ 7. Let your mind breathe today.	**3** ♀♅⚷♆℞ 8. Count your blessings.
4 ♀♅⚷♆℞ PST Begins ☽-V/C 12:26 AM ☽→♎ 1:00 AM 9. Have gratitude for all.	**5** ♀♅⚷♆℞ 10. Looking forward supports awareness.	**6** ♀♅⚷♆℞ ☽-V/C 12:18 AM ☽→♏ 5:02 AM ♅→♈ 10:51 AM ☊→♋℞ 9:38 AM 11. Experience the vastness.	**7** ♀♅⚷♆℞ ● 15°♏11' - 8:01AM 3. Embrace life with joy.	**8** ♀♅⚷♆℞ ☽-V/C 2:41 AM ☽→♐ 10:59 AM ♃→♐ 4:39 AM 4. Beauty is order, manifest this.	**9** ♀♅⚷♆℞ ▲ 5. Change is progress, get moving.	**10** ♀♅⚷♆℞ ▲ ☽-V/C 7:34 PM ☽→♑ 7:54 PM 6. Recognize your beauty in many ways.
11 ♀♅⚷♆℞ ▲ Veteran's Day 7. Study the details to see the lesson.	**12** ♀♅⚷♆℞ 8. Increase your wealth with ease.	**13** ♀♅⚷♆℞ ☽-V/C 7:13 AM ☽→♒ 7:45 AM 9. Grow spiritually through service.	**14** ♀♅⚷♆℞ 10. Look for innovative ideas.	**15** ♀♅⚷♆℞ ☽-V/C 7:58 PM ☽→♓ 8:41 PM ♂→♓ 2:22 PM 11. Universal joy expands your view.	**16** ☿♅⚷♆℞ ♀S/D-25°♎14' - 2:52 PM ☿S/R-13°♐28' - 5:34 PM 3. Play a board game with some friends.	**17** ☿♅⚷♆℞ 4. Your practical side is comforting.
18 ☿♅⚷♆℞ ☽-V/C 2:03 AM ☽→♈ 7:55 AM 5. Expect an active and fast day.	**19** ☿♅⚷♆℞ 6. Beautiful music fills the soul.	**20** ☿♅⚷♆℞ ☽-V/C 2:46 PM ☽→♉ 3:42 PM 7. Know the truth.	**21** ☿♅⚷♆℞ 8. Give energy to your ambitions.	**22** ☿♅⚷♆℞ Thanksgiving Day ☽-V/C 1:58 AM ☽→♊ 8:10 PM ☉→♐ 1:03 AM ○ 0°♊52' - 9:39 PM 9. Heart connections are strong today.	**23** ☿♅⚷♆℞ 10. A wise person knows when to stop.	**24** ☿♅⚷℞ ▼ ☽-V/C 9:31 PM ☽→♋ 10:37 PM ♆S/D 13°♓41' - 5:10 PM 11. Be open to a mystical experience.
25 ☿♅⚷℞ ▼ 3. Optimism creates a fun holiday season.	**26** ☿♅⚷℞ ☽-V/C 11:21 PM 4. Make a plan for the rest of the year.	**27** ☿♅⚷℞ ☽→♌ 12:34 AM 5. Remain flexible.	**28** ☿♅⚷℞ 6. Be pure of heart.	**29** ☿♅⚷℞ ☽-V/C 1:46 AM ☽→♍ 3:07 AM 7. Let silence be your teacher.	**30** ☿♅⚷℞ 8. Celebrate your victories!	

♈ Aries	♎ Libra	☉ Sun	♄ Saturn	→ Enters	2. Balance	8. Money
♉ Taurus	♏ Scorpio	☽ Moon	♅ Uranus	℞ Retrograde	3. Fun	9. Spirituality
♊ Gemini	♐ Sagittarius	☿ Mercury	♆ Neptune	S/D Stationary Direct	4. Structure	10. Visionary
♋ Cancer	♑ Capricorn	♀ Venus	♇ Pluto	V/C Void-of-Course	5. Action	11. Completion
♌ Leo	♒ Aquarius	♂ Mars	⚷ Chiron	▲ Super Sensitivity	6. Love	
♍ Virgo	♓ Pisces	♃ Jupiter	☊ North Node	▼ Low Vitality	7. Learning	

New Moon in Scorpio

When the Sun is in Scorpio

Scorpio is the symbol of darkness which heralds the decline of the Sun in Autumn. Scorpio embodies the Law of Nature, which decrees that even the strongest will must bow to the body's mortality. As we watch all of nature going through a slow death, we begin to recognize the qualities of Scorpio's subtlety and depth, and the hidden forces that threaten those who live only on the surface. Scorpio rules all of the things that you try to keep hidden: death, taxes, power, money, sex, resentment, revenge, ambition, pride, and fear. When you face these self-imposed limits on yourself, you take on the true power of transformation. Transformation establishes pathways for you to decentralize the ego in the interest of higher humanitarian work.

Scorpio Goddess

Scorpio moons ask you to delve deep into your Soul. There's no better companion in this process than Inanna, who journeyed to the Underworld and relinquished her power and possessions, one-at-a-time at each of seven gates, until she was stripped bare to her essential self, without any trappings or embellishments.

Ask your soul sister Inanna to accompany you in a candle-lit meditation to release that which you no longer need to carry in each of your seven chakras. Let go of anything encumbering your essential self, anything weighing you down. Connect with the dark, cool Earth and tune into anything that you feel like you've put behind you, but might not have completely released. Allow Inanna to empty your backpack and lighten your load, so you can rise and be reborn anew.

Build Your Altar

Colors	Deep red, black, deep purple
Numerology	3 – Embrace life with joy
Tarot Card	Death – The ability to transform, transmute, and transcend
Gemstones	Topaz, smoky quartz, obsidian, jet, onyx
Plant Remedy	Manzanita – Being open to transforming cycles
Fragrance	Sandalwood – Awakens your sensuality

Moon Notes

November 7th, 8:01 AM

New Moon 15° Scorpio 11'
New moons are about manifestation, planting seeds, and becoming fruitful.

Statement	I Transform
Body	Sex organs
Mind	Investigation
Spirit	Transformation

Element
Water – Taking the path of least resistance, going with the flow, creativity at it's best. Secretive, glamourous, sensual, psychic, magnetic, actress, escape artist, and healer.

Choice Points

Light	Humaneness
Shadow	Insincere
Wisdom	Apply your knowledge innovatively.

Sabian Symbol
A girl's face breaking into a smile.

Potential
It's a sign of better days to come.

11th House Moon I Know/I Transform

Umbrella Energy
Your approach to friends, social consciousness, teamwork, community service, and the future.

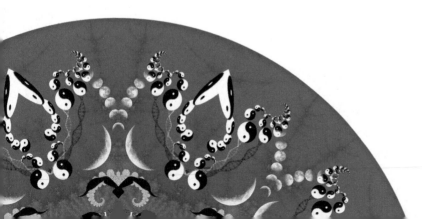

Scorpio Victories & Challenges

Say all of the statements in this section out loud. Then, underline the phrase that means the most to you. Use the phrase as your affirmation for recalibrating throughout this moon phase.

"When the student needs to learn, the teacher appears." Today, I recognize that the Law of Reflection is in operation. I have become aware of this through my over-indulgence of judgment and criticism of other people. I am aware that when my judgment is running rampant, I am in need of a teacher who can interpret this judgment as reflection, so I can see my judgments as my teachers and use them to re-interpret myself. I seek counsel with someone who has the ability to listen to me, hear me, and give me the space I need to see myself. I have become confused by spending too much time looking outside of myself for the answers. Perhaps my authority systems, like my religion or my family traditions, no longer serve me and I need to use this confusion to become aware of a new, more self-reliant way to live my life.

The Law of Reflection

Whatever I judge is what I am, what I fear, or what I lack. I make a list of my judgments:

I rewrite each judgment in the form of a question:
Am I _____? Do I fear _____? Do I lack _____?

Example 1: I judge Mary's wealth. Do I fear wealth? Do I lack wealth? Am I wealthy in my own way and forgetting to acknowledge my own ability to manifest?

Example 2: I judge John's "be perfect" attitude. Do I fear perfection? Do I lack perfection? Have I forgotten to recognize my own perfection?

In moving through this process, I reconnect to myself and find my own authority today. I send blessings to others whose reflection has so beautifully shown me myself today. I now know and cherish my judgments as my greatest teachers and set myself free today.

Scorpio Homework

Scorpios manifest best by being a private investigator, detective, probate attorney, mystery writer, mythologist, Tarot reader, symbolist, hospice worker, transition counselor, mortician, sex surrogate, or in forensic medicine.

The Scorpio moon cycle asks you to transform. In order to do this you must transmute sex drive into creativity, physical comfort into serving the greater good, money into higher value, fear into light, animosity into understanding, ambition into service to beauty, pride into humility, separation into unity, control into harmony, and power into empowerment.

Victory List

Acknowledge what you have overcome.
Keep this list active during this moon cycle.
Honoring victory allows you to accept success.

Sky Power Yoga

Seated Cat/Cow

You need one chair for the prop.

With your back straight sit one hand-width from the back of the chair with your feet on the floor hip-width apart. If your feet require more solid contact with the floor, place pillows or folded towels under your feet.

Sit comfortably with a straight back and gently cup knees. Breathe in and out slowly and deeply several times through your nose with your awareness on your reproductive organs.

Inhale and allow your belly to drop down as your pelvis tilts back into a subtle back bend.

As you inhale, say or think to yourself the mantra *I Transform*.

Exhale slowly as you tilt your pelvis forward and round your back slightly into a gentle forward bend while gazing down. Repeat with a smooth, continuous movement as many times as desired.

Manifesting List

Scorpio Manifesting Ideas

Now is the time to focus on manifesting transformation on all levels, bringing light to the dark, knowing and living cycles, knowing trust as an option, accepting change, accepting my sexuality, knowing sex is natural, knowing sex as good, and knowing sex as creative.

This or something better than this comes to me in an easy and pleasurable way, for the good of all concerned. Thank you, Universe!

209

New Moon in Scorpio

Your Personal Moon Experience

Fill in the Cosmic Check-In page. Then look up the degree of the Moon on the chart below. Take note of the "I" statement on the outside of the wheel where the Moon is located. Now, locate the same degree on your own chart and make a note of the house and corresponding "I" statement. Go back to the Cosmic Check-In page and circle the two statements from the charts and read what you wrote. This will give you an idea about what to expect from this moon phase on a personal level. For more information on personalizing your *Moon Book*, go to www.BlueMoonAcademy.com and look for *How to Use the Moon Book*.

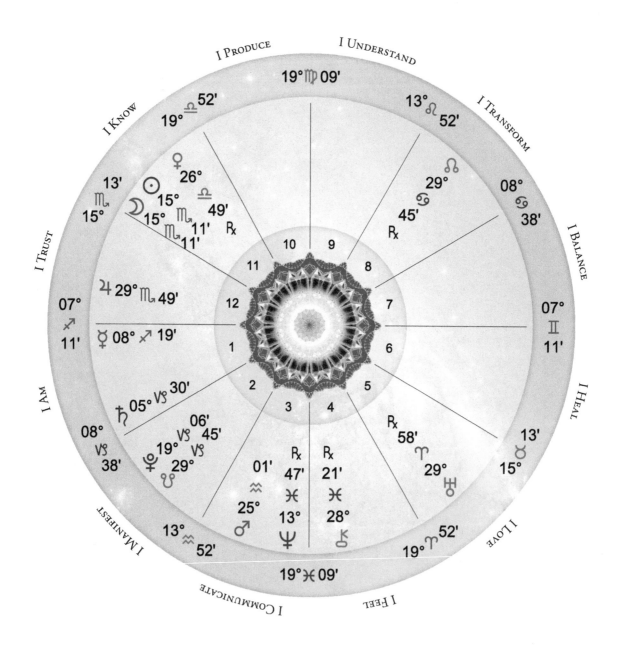

	Aries		Cancer		Scorpio		Pisces		Venus		Uranus		North Node
	Taurus		Leo		Sagittarius		Sun		Mars		Neptune		South Node
	Gemini		Virgo		Capricorn		Moon		Jupiter		Pluto		Retrograde
			Libra		Aquarius		Mercury		Saturn		Chiron		

Cosmic Check-in

Scorpio New Moon
November 7th
8:01 AM

Take a moment to write a brief phrase for each "I" statement.
This activates all areas of your life for this creative cycle.

♏ I Transform

♐ I Understand

♑ I Produce

♒ I Know

♓ I Trust

♈ I Am

♉ I Manifest

♊ I Communicate

♋ I Feel

♌ I Love

♍ I Heal

♎ I Balance

Full Moon in Gemini

When the Sun is Opposite the Moon

Full moons are always in opposition to the Sun. This creates a feeling of tension between where you want to shine and how your feelings are flowing on a sensory level about the Sun's directive. The two forces seem like they are working against each other, yet they are on the same team displaying different techniques to obtain the same mission. The Gemini/Sagittarius polarity creates tension between community ideas and global thinking.

Gemini Goddess

Saraswati beckons you to withdraw from the party scene and into the quiet, contemplative process to dream your finest creations into being. Goddess of all creative endeavors: writing, art, dance, and music, Saraswati can assist you in your waking hours and in the dreamtime.

Get out your crayons, markers, paints, and pastels, and create a massive mind map with your happiness and fulfillment at the core (your new seedpod). What sprouts from the center? What branches off? Trust the process to generate ideas to rebirth you into joyful action! Post the map where you will see it often so it can serve as an active reminder of who you are and where you're headed!

Build Your Altar

Colors	Bright yellow, orange, multi-colors
Numerology	9 – Heart connections are strong today
Tarot Card	Lovers – Connecting to wholeness
Gemstones	Yellow diamond, citrine, yellow jade, yellow topaz
Plant remedy	Morning Glory – Thinking with your heart, not your head
Fragrance	Iris – The ability to focus the mind

Moon Notes

November 22nd, 9:39 PM

Full Moon 0° Gemini 52'
Full Moons are about releasing, letting go, becoming free, and recalibrating.

Statement	I Communicate
Body	Lungs and hands
Mind	Academic
Spirit	Intelligence

Element
Air – The breath of life that allows the mind to achieve new insights and fresh perspectives, inspiration, active and abstract dreaming, and freedom from attachments.

Choice Points

Light	Lucidity
Shadow	Indecisive
Wisdom	Make room for something new in your life.

Sabian Symbol
A glass-bottomed boat reveals undersea wonders.

Potential
Knowing the message is beneath the surface.

10th House Moon
I Produce/I Communicate

Umbrella Energy
Your approach to status, career, honor, and prestige, and why you chose your Father.

Karmic Awakening
Aries/Libra – It's "I" versus "We," codependent versus independent.

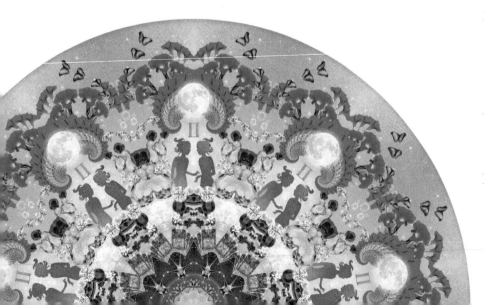

Clearing the Slate

Sixty hours before the full moon negative traits connected to the astro-sign might become activated to trigger what needs to be released during the full moon phase. You may notice that you are not listening to others and overriding what others are saying by talking too much. Watch out for gossiping or omitting the truth. Make a list, look in the mirror, and for each negative trait, tell yourself *I am sorry, I forgive you, thank you for your awareness,* and *I love you.*

Gemini Victories & Challenges

Say all of the statements in this section out loud. Then, underline the phrase that means the most to you. Use the phrase as your affirmation for recalibrating throughout this moon phase.

Today, I blend my old self with my new self, my physical reality with my spiritual awareness, my positive thoughts with my negative thoughts, my past with my present, my feminine with my masculine, my rewards with my losses, my ups with my downs, and my higher self with my lower self. It is a day for me to refine and fine tune my life by looking at my extremes. I recognize what inspires me and what keeps me stuck. I find my center today by acknowledging my extremes. I am aware that balance comes to those who are able to locate the space in the center of these opposite energy fields.

When I am in my center, my polarities are in motion. Healing cannot occur unless my polarities are moving and I know that healing is motion. I am ready for a healing today. I know that by visiting my opposites, and determining their vast opposition to each other, I can find the paradoxes that I have chosen for myself and begin to heal. I am willing to experiment with this blending of opposites and become the alchemist of my own life. When I blend all aspects of myself, rather than separating them, I can truly become whole. Today is a day to integrate, rather than separate, in order to release the spark of light that stays prisoner when my polarities are in operation. When I find balance, motion occurs and the Law of Harmony takes over, putting paradoxical energies to rest, thus breaking the crystallization of polarity. The Law of Harmony is beauty in motion and promotes the flow of color, light, sound, and movement into form. Balance is a condition that keeps my spark in motion. I become the vertical line in the center of polarity today and carry the secret of balance. Balance cannot be my goal; motion is my goal today. When I am in motion, I can take action to evolve and to express all of myself freely.

Gemini Homework

Sit still and invite silence into your space. Stay quiet and still for at least 5 minutes. During this time take an inventory and see where you have interrupted people in the middle of their sentences. Now is the time to make a conscious effort to allow others the space to express their thoughts. Keep sitting in silence and feel the frustration, while embracing the power of silence.

Gratitude List

Keep this list active throughout the moon cycle. This will bring you to a level of completion so that a new cycle of opportunity can occur in your life. Be prepared for miracles!

Sky Power Yoga

Reclined Heart Opener

You need two bath towels and one to two pillows for the prop.

Fold two towels in half lengthwise, roll them into a log, and place them on the floor. Put both pillows on top of the rolled towels to support your back, neck, and head in the pose.

Sit on the floor with the support prop behind you.

Lean back onto your elbows and then lower your back onto your support prop. This creates a gentle opening across your chest. If you find your head dangling over the top edge, shift your prop towards your head to support your head and neck fully.

Place your arms out at a 45-degree angle with palms facing upward at your sides.

Relax.   Close your eyes. Breathe in and out slowly and deeply several times through your nose keeping your awareness on your lungs and hands.

Inhale and keep your awareness on the expansion of your lungs. Exhale softly and slowly as you say or think to yourself the mantra *I Communicate*.

Relax fully into the support prop and the pose. Enjoy breathing with the mantra for a few minutes.

Freedom List

Say this statement out loud three times before writing your list:

I am a free spiritual being and it is my desire to be free to think and to express myself fully.

Gemini
Recalibrating Ideas

Now is the time to activate a game change in my life, and give up my attitude about unfinished business, shallow communication, old files and office clutter, broken communication devices, lies I tell myself, temptation to gossip, restlessness, over-thinking, and vacillation.

From this day forward I resolve to be true — first to myself and my highest self, and then to the highest self in me which is the Source of Love That I Am.

217

Full Moon in Gemini

Your Personal Moon Experience

Fill in the Cosmic Check-In page. Then look up the degree of the Moon on the chart below. Take note of the "I" statement on the outside of the wheel where the Moon is located. Now, locate the same degree on your own chart and make

a note of the house and corresponding "I" statement. Go back to the Cosmic Check-In page, circle the two statements from the charts, and read what you wrote. This will give you an idea about what to expect from this moon phase on a personal level. For a personalized *My Moon Experience* Astrology reading with Beatrex, go to www.beatrex.com.

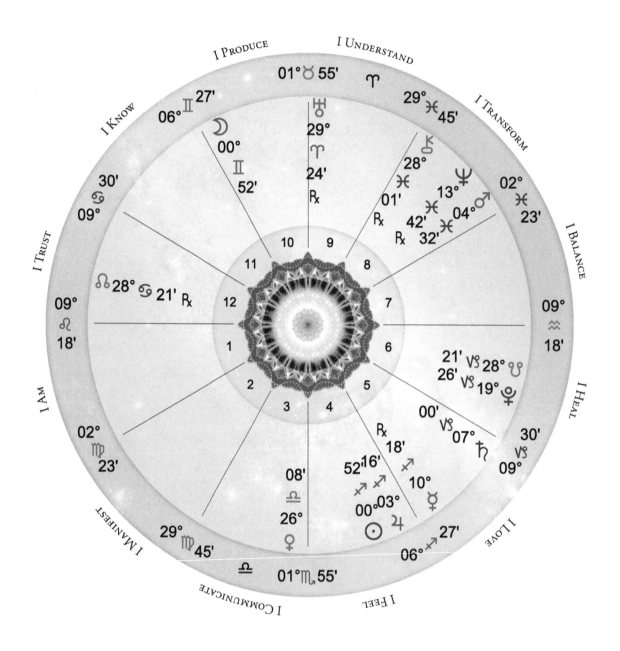

♈ Aries	♋ Cancer	♏ Scorpio	♓ Pisces	♀ Venus	♅ Uranus	☊ North Node
♉ Taurus	♌ Leo	♐ Sagittarius	☉ Sun	♂ Mars	♆ Neptune	☋ South Node
♊ Gemini	♍ Virgo	♑ Capricorn	☽ Moon	♃ Jupiter	♇ Pluto	℞ Retrograde
	♎ Libra	♒ Aquarius	☿ Mercury	♄ Saturn	⚷ Chiron	

Cosmic Check-in

Gemini Full Moon
November 22nd
9:39 PM

Take a moment to write a brief phrase for each "I" statement.
This activates all areas of your life for this creative cycle.

♊ I Communicate

♋ I Feel

♌ I Love

♍ I Heal

♎ I Balance

♏ I Transform

♐ I Understand

♑ I Produce

♒ I Know

♓ I Trust

♈ I Am

♉ I Manifest

December

December 1: Mercury retrograde backs into Scorpio

This is the time to be a private eye. Investigation is at the top of the priority list with this transit. Anything you try to keep secret will come out and be revealed. Don't even try.

December 2: Venus enters Scorpio

Sensuality is the name of the game right now. Venus is impulsive so know that anything can develop into a deep connection at a moment's notice. Enjoy yourself.

December 3-6: Pluto conjunct South Node in Capricorn opposite North Node in Cancer

Pluto and the North Node are working overtime to promote letting go, transformation, and recalibration of what no longer serves us. All outdated things, people, and concepts will be moved into the obsolete file. Be willing and experience the freedom that comes with this. The other half of this opposition is the North Node (our future) connecting to Cancer, expect this to bring new focus to our country and innovation to the ideas of home and family.

December 6: Mercury goes direct in Scorpio

This is a fabulous energy field to express fully what has been placed in your shadow. Consciousness helps you open to an advancement in intuitive nature.

December 6-10: Neptune conjunct Mars in Pisces

This is a strong focus on advancement at an intuitive level. Be cautious to balance your 'out-of-body' activity with your 'physical-body' activity to avoid accidents. On the other hand, action could really assist in manifesting a dream come true. Go for it!

December 7-9, 19-20: Super Sensitivity

The gateway to the cosmos is open to us right now on many levels so expect a major download. Be sure to keep careful boundaries open around you so you can receive in a gentle and graceful manner.

December 12: Mercury enters Sagittarius

Time to realize that there is a major enhancement in the 'Intelligence Codes.' Both sides of the brain are in operation on an expanded level. Now is the time to write that book, start that empowering lecture series, or create that new game you have thought about for years.

December 21: Sun enters Capricorn – Winter Solstice

Once again we celebrate the advancement of light merging with the dark waters of life, celebrating the Earth's Birthday. Light a candle and place essential oil on your wrist to open your soul to the acceptance of the new light.

December 21-23: Low Vitality

Monitor your energy. If you feel tired, rest and take a nap. Exhaustion can take you out of the game. Be aware, drink water, and let things simply BE.

Sunday	Monday	Tuesday	Wednesday	Thursday	Friday	Saturday
						1 ☿♅⚷℞ ☽-V/C 6:34 AM ☽→♎ 6:48 AM ☿→♏ 3:13 AM 9. Let your spirit soar.
2 ☿♅⚷℞ ♀→♏ 9:03 AM 10. Notice the creativity in innovation.	**3** ☿♅⚷℞ Hanukkah ☽-V/C 10:15 AM ☽→♏ 11:54 AM 11. Expand your horizons.	**4** ☿♅⚷℞ 3. Feel your heart filled with joy.	**5** ☿♅⚷℞ ☽-V/C 1:53 PM ☽→♐ 6:48 PM 4. Be aware of your ground state.	**6** ♅⚷℞ ● 15°♐7′ - 11:20 PM ☿ S/D-27°♏17′ 1:23 PM 5. Use cleverness and enjoy life.	**7** ♅⚷℞ ▲ 6. Set the stage for romance.	**8** ♅⚷℞ ▲ ☽-V/C 2:00 AM ☽→♑ 4:01 AM 7. Discover Divinity in the details.
9 ♅⚷℞ ▲ 8. Buy yourself the first gift.	**10** ♅⚷℞ ☽-V/C 1:26 PM ☽→♒ 3:39 PM 9. Let spiritual grace comfort you.	**11** ♅⚷℞ 10. Be on the leading edge of the wedge.	**12** ♅⚷℞ ☿→♐ 3:44 PM 11. The vastness is motivating.	**13** ♅⚷℞ ☽-V/C 2:19 AM ☽→♓ 4:39 AM 3. Believe in yourself.	**14** ♅⚷℞ 4. Get to the post office early.	**15** ♅⚷℞ ☽-V/C 3:49 AM ☽→♈ 4:44 PM 5. Plan your New Year's vacation.
16 ♅⚷℞ 6. Light up your life.	**17** ♅⚷℞ ☽-V/C 11:21 PM 7. Write a holiday story.	**18** ♅⚷℞ ☽→♉ 1:37 AM 8. Let the gold dust guide you.	**19** ♅⚷℞ ▲ ☽-V/C 4:41 PM 9. Be heart connected.	**20** ♅⚷℞ ▲ ☽→♊ 6:34 AM 10. Open your heart, dream big.	**21** ♅⚷℞ ▼ ☉→♑-2:24 PM Winter Solstice 2. Balance with diversity.	**22** ♅⚷℞ ▼ ☽-V/C 6:20 AM ☽→♋ 8:27 AM ○ 0°♋49′ - 9:48 AM 3. Honor your ancestors.
23 ♅⚷℞ ▼ 4. Stand firmly in place.	**24** ♅⚷℞ ☽-V/C 6:50 AM ☽→♌ 8:58 AM 5. Walk off your holiday dinner.	**25** ♅⚷℞ Christmas Day 6. Merry Christmas. Live love.	**26** ♅⚷℞ ☽-V/C 7:36 AM ☽→♍ 9:49 AM 7. Think clearly now.	**27** ♅⚷℞ 8. Celebrate abundance.	**28** ♅⚷℞ ☽-V/C 8:26 AM ☽→♎ 12:22 PM 9. Support your favorite cause.	**29** ♅⚷℞ 10. Have faith in your future.
30 ♅⚷℞ ☽-V/C 2:53 PM ☽→♏ 5:22 PM 11. Reach completion with a full heart.	**31** ♅⚷℞ 3. Happy New Year! Celebrate!					

♈ Aries	♍ Virgo	♓ Pisces	♃ Jupiter	➡ Enters	2. Balance	8. Money
♉ Taurus	♎ Libra	☉ Sun	♄ Saturn	℞ Retrograde	3. Fun	9. Spirituality
♊ Gemini	♏ Scorpio	☽ Moon	♅ Uranus	S/D Stationary Direct	4. Structure	10. Visionary
♋ Cancer	♐ Sagittarius	☿ Mercury	♆ Neptune	V/C Void-of-Course	5. Action	11. Completion
♌ Leo	♑ Capricorn	♀ Venus	♇ Pluto	▲ Super Sensitivity	6. Love	
	♒ Aquarius	♂ Mars	⚷ Chiron	▼ Low Vitality	7. Learning	

New Moon in Sagittarius

When the Sun is in Sagittarius

Now is the time for greater expansion of consciousness. Sagittarius is about exterminating all of the man-eating symbols of our illusions, harmful thoughts, inertia, prejudices, and superstitions that hide behind our excuses. It is truth time, so that the Soul Goal of the Sagittarius can come into being and direct its light toward greater aspiration. Questions to ask yourself at this time are: What is my goal for myself? What is my goal for my nation? What is my goal for humanity? All goals get stimulated during this time.

Sagittarius Goddess

Let Persephone, who chose to stay in the Underworld half of the year and became the Queen of Death, be your guide as you enter the dark time of the year. Harvest is over and you now allow the land to become fallow – plowed, but unseeded. Persephone, in the version of the myth unspoiled by patriarchy, hears the cries of those stuck in purgatory, and is moved to voluntarily guide the anguished toward the completion of their spiritual journeys.

Of Persephone, also known as the maiden Kore, Plato wrote, "She is wise and touches that which is in motion." Where might you be stuck and how can Persephone get you moving in the right direction? What in your life do you seek to transform? Who do you wish to become?

Build Your Altar

Colors	Deep purple, deep blue, turquoise
Numerology	5 – Use cleverness and enjoy life
Tarot Card	Temperance – Blending physical and spiritual
Gemstones	Turquoise, lapis
Plant Remedy	Madia – Seeing the target and hitting it
Fragrance	Magnolia – Expanded beauty

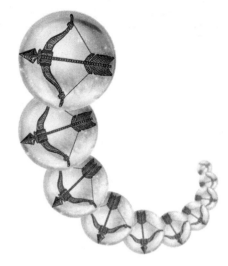

Moon Notes

December 6th, 11:20 PM

New Moon 15° Sagittarius 07'
New moons are about manifestation, planting seeds, and becoming fruitful.

Statement	I Understand
Body	Thighs
Mind	Philosophical
Spirit	Inspiration

Element
Earth – Practical, determined, structured, enduring, stubborn, traditional, stable, and stuck inside the box.

Choice Points

Light	Watchfulness
Shadow	Excitability
Wisdom	Your sensitivity detects changes in Earth's energy flows.

Sabian Symbol
Sea Gulls fly around a ship looking for food.

Potential
Spending time going for the easy way out diminishes self-worth.

4th House Moon I Feel/I Understand

Umbrella Energy
The way your early environmental training was and how that set your foundation for living, and why you chose your mother.

Sagittarius Victories & Challenges

Sagittarius New Moon
December 6th
11:20 PM

Say all of the statements in this section out loud. Then, underline the phrase that means the most to you. Use the phrase as your affirmation for recalibrating throughout this moon phase.

Destiny is in my favor today. I know, without a doubt, that I cannot make a wrong turn today. I access my blueprint to ensure perfect timing for all opportunities to be open to me today. I promise to be open to these opportunities, knowing full well that today is my day. I am on time and in time today. My destiny is here and working in my favor. I see all that is available to me today and claim my pathway to success. I pay attention to what comes my way today and know that it is an opening for good fortune to be my reality. I am ready to accept my good fortune now. All I have to do is move in the direction of my truth. I know that my truth is my good fortune. I trust in coincidence and synchronicity to provide me with direction to my destiny. All points of action lead me to my true expression. I can see clearly into my future today with great optimism. I intend it. I allow it. So be it. All is in Divine Order.

Mantra during this Time *(repeat this 10 times out loud)*

"My truth is my good fortune. My timing is perfect. I trust that all that comes to me today is in my highest and best good. I am open to optimism. The drum of destiny beats in my favor. So be it!"

Sagittarius Homework

Sagittarians manifest best through teaching, publishing and writing, travel, spiritual adventures, and as tour group leaders, airline and cruise ship personnel, evangelical ministers, philosophers, anthropologists, linguists, and translators.

The Sagittarius moon cycle creates a magnetic matrix that stimulates us to take direction towards becoming one with a goal and then sheds light on the path. In the ancient mystery schools, Sagittarius moons were used to set the stage for candidates to reach higher levels of awareness by inspiring their desire to reach a goal and then to step toward the goal. It is time now to become one with your goal.

Victory List

Acknowledge what you have overcome.
Keep this list active during this moon cycle.
Honoring victory allows you to accept success.

Sky Power Yoga

Reclined Windshield Wipers

No prop is needed.

Lay on the floor face up with your legs bent and feet on the floor hip-width apart. Place arms out at your sides with palms facing down.

Relax. Close your eyes. Breathe in and out slowly and deeply several times through your nose with your awareness on your thighs. To create the windshield wipers movement, rock both your knees to the left and then to the right.

Connect the movement with your breath—inhale and move knees to the left and exhale moving knees to the right.

Inhale softly as you say or think to yourself the mantra *I Understand* and move your legs to the left.

Exhale softly and move legs right. Repeat as desired.

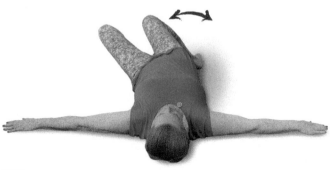 

Manifesting List

Sagittarius Manifesting Ideas

Now is the time to focus on manifesting truth, teaching and study, understanding advanced ideas, optimism and inspiration, bliss, goals, travel and adventure, and philosophy and culture.

This or something better than this comes to me in an easy and pleasurable way, for the good of all concerned. Thank you, Universe!

New Moon in Sagittarius

Your Personal Moon Experience

Fill in the Cosmic Check-In page. Then look up the degree of the Moon on the chart below. Take note of the "I" statement on the outside of the wheel where the Moon is located. Now, locate the same degree on your own chart and make a note of the house and corresponding "I" statement. Go back to the Cosmic Check-In page and circle the two statements from the charts and read what you wrote. This will give you an idea about what to expect from this moon phase on a personal level. For more information on personalizing your *Moon Book*, go to www.BlueMoonAcademy.com and look for *How to Use the Moon Book*.

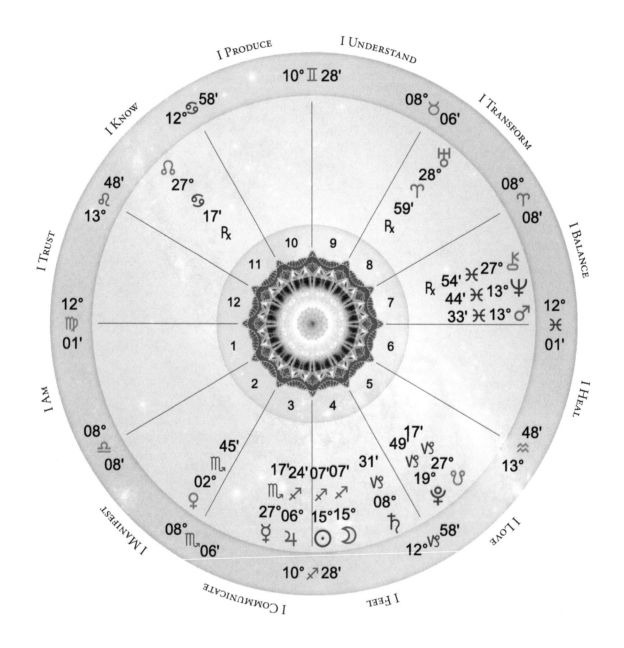

♈	Aries	♋	Cancer	♏	Scorpio	♓	Pisces	♀	Venus	♅	Uranus	☊	North Node
♉	Taurus	♌	Leo	♐	Sagittarius	☉	Sun	♂	Mars	♆	Neptune	☋	South Node
♊	Gemini	♍	Virgo	♑	Capricorn	☽	Moon	♃	Jupiter	♇	Pluto	℞	Retrograde
		♎	Libra	♒	Aquarius	☿	Mercury	♄	Saturn	⚷	Chiron		

Cosmic Check-in

Sagittarius New Moon
December 6th
11:20 PM

Take a moment to write a brief phrase for each "I" statement.
This activates all areas of your life for this creative cycle.

♐ I Understand

♑ I Produce

♒ I Know

♓ I Trust

♈ I Am

♉ I Manifest

♊ I Communicate

♋ I Feel

♌ I Love

♍ I Heal

♎ I Balance

♏ I Transform

Full Moon in Cancer

When the Sun is Opposite the Moon

Full moons are always in opposition to the Sun. This creates a feeling of tension between where you want to shine and how your feelings are flowing on a sensory level about the Sun's directive. The two forces seem like they are working against each other, yet they are on the same team displaying different techniques to obtain the same mission. The Cancer/Capricorn polarity creates tension between being at home with your family or being at work positioning yourself for success.

Cancer Goddess

Birds are the symbol of expanded consciousness because they are born twice; once into the egg and once out of the egg. They are associated with rebirth and self-realization. Bird Woman is the Cancer goddess. She teaches us that, although we live in the illusion that security comes from our identity in the outer world, our true cosmic significance must be found within. Bird Woman directs us toward discovering our way home to our Soul, the place of lotus light. She has the ability to fly between Heaven and Earth, bringing communications from the angels and the spirit guides. She inspires souls to infuse matter with light—the true essence of co-creating.

Build Your Altar

Colors Shades of gray and milky, creamy colors

Numerology 3 – Honor your ancestors

Tarot Card The Chariot – The ability to move forward

Gemstones Pearl, moonstone, ruby

Plant Remedy Shooting Star – The ability to move straight ahead

Fragrance Peppermint – The essence of the Great Mother

Moon Notes

December 22nd, 9:48 AM

Full Moon 0° Cancer 49'
  Full Moons are about releasing, letting go, becoming free, and recalibrating.

Statement I Feel

Body Breast

Mind Security

Spirit Building form

Element
  Water – Taking the path of least resistance, going with the flow, creativity at its best. Secretive, glamourous, sensual, psychic, magnetic, actress, escape artist, and healer.

Dropping Moon
  Write your intentions early, before the Moon goes void.

Choice Points
  Light   Adaptability
  Shadow   Instability
  Wisdom   Clarify what you have available to give.

Sabian Symbol
  On a ship the sailors lower an old flag and raise a new one.

Potential
  Changing of loyalties and announcing new standards.

5th House Moon I Love/I Feel

Umbrella Energy
  The way you love and how you want to be loved.

Karmic Awakening
  Pisces/Virgo – Nature healing versus allopathic healing.

Clearing the Slate

Sixty hours before the full moon, negative traits connected to the astro-sign might become activated to trigger what needs to be released during the full moon phase. You may notice an unusual amount of worry, moodiness, addiction to the past, or challenges related to the energy of mothering. Make a list, look in the mirror, and for each negative trait, tell yourself *I am sorry, I forgive you, thank you for your awareness,* and *I love you.*

Cancer Victories & Challenges

Say all of the statements in this section out loud. Then, underline the phrase that means the most to you. Use the phrase as your affirmation for recalibrating throughout this moon phase.

Today, I take advantage of my ability to take action and position myself for success. I clearly know that the road to success is before me, and all I need to do is move forward. I am aware that when I take action and move forward, the Universe fills in the dots. Whether I move left, right, or straight ahead doesn't matter—what matters is that I am in movement. Today, I release indecisiveness that keeps me stuck. Today, I let go of vacillation that exhausts my mind. Today, I take my foot off of the brakes and find the gas pedal. I allow movement to occur, even if I don't know where I am going. When I take action, I trust the guideposts will appear. I am aware that action leads me to my new direction. Today, I know and GO! I remember that Karma comes to the space of non-action, while success comes through action. Action brings me to my victory. Standing still leads to regret, resentment, and chaos. I am aware that action can be as simple as taking a walk on the beach, buying fresh flowers to add a new dimension to my home, or simply going to a new restaurant for lunch. I take action today to break up a crystallized pattern and, in so doing, my life begins to show me newfound awareness and light to guide me.

Cancer Homework

It's now time to conquer pride and ambition, overcome fear of loneliness, release the need for money, security, and possessions, discover the value of emotions, and connect to beauty. Submerge yourself in a tub of water, relax, and let the clean water flow through your cells to wash away all of your hurts, resentments, and history that keep you trapped in the past. Pull the plug and let the spiral of water carry away your pain. Be prepared to boldly claim your presence in the present. Look around your kitchen and throw away the pots and pans that continue to feed your past, rather than vitalizing your life now.

Gratitude List

Keep this list active throughout the moon cycle. This will bring you to a level of completion so that a new cycle of opportunity can occur in your life. Be prepared for miracles!

 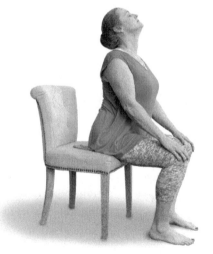 

Sky Power Yoga

Seated Cat/Cow

You need one chair for the prop.

With your back straight sit one hand-width from the back of the chair with your feet on the floor hip-width apart. If your feet require more solid contact with the floor, place pillows or folded towels under your feet.

Sit comfortably with a straight back and gently cup knees. Breathe in and out slowly and deeply several times through your nose with your awareness on your breasts.

Inhale and allow your belly to drop down as your pelvis tilts back into a subtle back bend.

As you inhale, say or think to yourself the mantra *I Feel*.

Exhale slowly as you tilt your pelvis forward and round your back slightly into a gentle forward bend while gazing down. Repeat with a smooth, continuous movement as many times as desired.

Freedom List

Say this statement out loud three times before writing your list:

I am a free spiritual being and it is my desire to be free to think and to express myself fully — to move about my life toward Truth and Wisdom — to accept and enjoy all good which is mine in living my truth.

Cancer Freedom Ideas

Now is the time to set myself free from self-pity, defensive behavior, nurturing everyone else but me, living in the past, being a mother, and having a mother.

I am now free and ready to make choices beyond survival!

Full Moon in Cancer

Your Personal Moon Experience

Fill in the Cosmic Check-In page. Then look up the degree of the Moon on the chart below. Take note of the "I" statement on the outside of the wheel where the Moon is located. Now, locate the same degree on your own chart and make

a note of the house and corresponding "I" statement. Go back to the Cosmic Check-In page, circle the two statements from the charts, and read what you wrote. This will give you an idea about what to expect from this moon phase on a personal level. For a personalized *My Moon Experience* Astrology reading with Beatrex, go to www.beatrex.com.

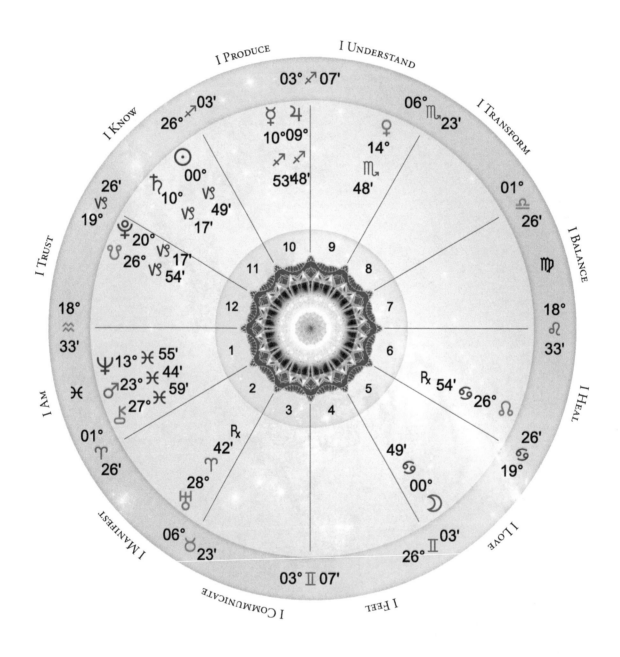

♈	Aries	♋	Cancer	♏	Scorpio	♓	Pisces	♀	Venus	♅	Uranus	☊	North Node
♉	Taurus	♌	Leo	♐	Sagittarius	☉	Sun	♂	Mars	♆	Neptune	☋	South Node
♊	Gemini	♍	Virgo	♑	Capricorn	☽	Moon	♃	Jupiter	♇	Pluto	℞	Retrograde
		♎	Libra	♒	Aquarius	☿	Mercury	♄	Saturn	⚷	Chiron		

Cosmic Check-in

Cancer Full Moon
December 22nd
9:48 AM

Take a moment to write a brief phrase for each "I" statement.
This activates all areas of your life for this creative cycle.

♋ I Feel

♌ I Love

♍ I Heal

♎ I Balance

♏ I Transform

♐ I Understand

♑ I Produce

♒ I Know

♓ I Trust

♈ I Am

♉ I Manifest

♊ I Communicate

About the Author

Beatrex Quntanna

Tarot expert, published author, symbolist, poet, lecturer—Beatrex is one of the luminaries of our time. Synthesizing more than 40 years of spiritual teachings, intuitive skills, and conventional counseling, she translates this wealth of wisdom into practical language making it accessible to all and applicable in today's world. Known for being "the teacher's teacher," her experience and advice has served as an invaluable support for many of today's spiritual teachers and professional psychics. She guides with profound insight, compassion for the human experience, and humor; inspiring personal growth and activating an inner-knowing in her students that sparks a self-confidence to walk tall in this world as a spiritual being.

Her life's work is showing how to Live Love Every Day by *living* astrology, not just intellectualizing it—teaching others how to ebb and flow with the natural cycles of the Moon and the cosmos, rather than working against them. She teaches this through Moon Classes held regularly throughout the year, and is the creator of *Living by the Light of the Moon*, a popular annual workbook that takes you step-by-step through her process.

Beatrex has written the ultimate book on the Tarot and its symbols, *Tarot: A Universal Language*, which has been reviewed by magazines in Europe as well as in the United States. She is the creator and co-presenter of the popular Annual Tarot Workshop with Michael Makay, designed as a complete support system to enhance your understanding of how best to work with the transformative energies of the upcoming year.

Beatrex's many print credits, as well as numerous radio, TV, and video appearances include:

- Regular guest blogger for Satiama.com and True Nature Healing Arts
- Contributing author to two anthologies by Maria Yracébûrû – *Prophetic Voices* and *Ah-Kine Remembrance*
- Monthly guest on *Spirit Seeker Hour* with host Cynde Meyer – tune in to *Spirit Seeker Magazine's* internet radio show on the first Tuesday of each month to get a free psychic mini-reading
- *Cosmic Check-In with Beatrex Quntanna* – a monthly YouTube show produced by Boyd Martin
- NEW *How to Use the Moon Book* online video course produced by Blue Moon Academy
- NEW *Tarot: A Universal Language* online course produced by Blue Moon Academy

Beatrex teaches ongoing astrology classes, facilitates a regular meditation group, and continues to be available for private group workshops in Encinitas, California.

Interested in...

- Ongoing Moon Classes and workshops with Beatrex?
- Personalized My Moon Experience astrological readings?

Contact her at beatrex@cox.net
or visit **www.Beatrex.com**

Other Works by Beatrex

The Year of Illumination 2018 — Wall Calendar

Created by Beatrex Quntanna and Michael Makay

With art and design by Jennifer Masters

According to Tibetan Numerology 2018 is an 11 Year

When first contemplating this year, Beatrex saw a vision of DNA strands circling in bright lights. The lights contained all the numbers and planets within the boundaries of the geometry. This became the inspiration for the Year 2018.

When we reach the number eleven, the Universe makes a cycle of completion and gateways open to a space of wonder. When something is complete it reaches a level of perfection. We all receive a recalibration of refinement and illumination that holds space in eternity. It is something quite wonderful when all is included and nothing is left out. The challenges in numerology become blessings under the umbrella of eleven. This allows for all that has been created to be renewed in the space of eternity and infinity, illuminated in vastness. We must accept the embrace of this enhanced height and width by opening to all the surprises that come forth and are presented to us. Spend time this year holding your arms out wide as a symbol of capturing assigned and un-assigned fields of energy. This establishes pathways flowing to you so the fulfillment of the year's promise can be yours.

Our 2018 calendar gives you insight into:

- **Astrological Highlights** that are easy to integrate into your life
- **Daily Intentions** based on Tibetan numerology by Michael Makay
- **Monthly Planetary Retrogrades** to keep you on track
- **Super-Sensitivity** and **Low-Vitality** days to assist in preventing accidents, burnout, and exhaustion
- **New, Full, and Void Moons** by time, astro-sign, and degree and the Sun's movement through the zodiac calculated by Katherine Sale

"*The Moon Book Calendar* has become an indispensable tool in my spiritual journey. Simple and easy to use, the calendar has helped me to understand and work with the cycles of the Sun, Moon and Stars to live a life of greater joy."

— Robin Simmons

"I consult *The Moon Book Calendar* to know when to make decisions, when to back up my computer, when to go to bed and rest, when to schedule classes, when it's good to begin projects, or travel. I use it to stay sane when I'm feeling low energy and see from the calendar that it's not just me! I have two calendars—one at home and one at work because the information is that important!"

— Kaliani Cynthia Hupper

To order, call 1-760-944-6020 or go to www.Beatrex.com

Tarot: A Universal Language

By Beatrex Quntanna

Experiencing the Road of Life Through Symbols

Embark on this fascinating journey through the unfolding Story of Life as told by the Universal Language of the Tarot. This book contains innovative avenues to understand the tarot through the author's in-depth knowledge of symbology.

Learn how to quickly read and interpret the Tarot by following this simple, informative, and illustrated guide. Use the expanded symbology section to understand each symbol depicted on the Minor and Major Arcana cards.

This book includes an interpretation of all 78 Tarot cards, plus readings created by this nationally-known Tarot teacher, reader, and symbolist.

To order, call 1-760-944-6020 or go to www.Beatrex.com

"I highly recommend Beatrex's Tarot: A Universal Language *for getting quick and easy-to-relate-to interpretations of the cards, as well as a very wonderful glossary of the different symbols on each card. It's really great that the book is printed in full color."*
— MICHELENNE CRAB, TAROT READER

Tarot: A Universal Language Online Course

With Beatrex Quntanna

Experience the amazing interpretation and wisdom behind each and every Tarot card from Beatrex. This course is now available online for the first time ever. Beatrex has over forty years of experience giving Tarot readings and teaching the Tarot to her students.

Now this wealth of knowledge is available to you to study at your leisure.

The course includes:

- High-quality instructional videos
- Study aids
- Fun quizzes
- Insightful activities

Whether you are on a journey to learn the Tarot for your own enlightenment or whether you want to do Tarot card readings for others, this is the course for you. Beatrex fills the course with her insightful wisdom, funny stories, and deep, anchored knowledge of the Tarot. Don't miss this course.

In this online course you will...

- Get to know the meanings and symbols of the Tarot cards
- Understand how to increase your intuition by using the cards
- Receive special reading spreads appropriate for different issues
- Meditate with the cards—let the symbols speak to you
- Learn how to set up a vortex in your office for doing readings
- Understand how to care for and treat your Tarot deck

Blue Moon Academy

For more information or to enroll now, go to
www.BlueMoonAcademy.com

How to Use the Moon Book Online Course

With Beatrex Quntanna

Everything you need to know about using the *Living by the Light of the Moon* workbook to create magic and abundance in your life!

Online! Enroll and Start Learning Now

The Moon is the great cosmic architect, the builder and the dissolver of form. Full Moons are about dissolving obstacles and outdated patterns so you can become free. New Moons are about co-creating, accepting, and receiving what you want in your life.

How to navigate your life by the light of the Moon and its cycles, *Living by the Light of the Moon*, also known to Beatrex's students as "The Moon Book", is an annual workbook that will show you step-by-step when and what to do to free yourself from whatever holds you back, and when and what to co-create.

Following along with this video class series helps you understand how to use the workbook easily and effortlessly.

The course includes:

- High-quality instructional videos on each aspect of the book
- A handout that makes it easy to follow along
- And the warmth and wisdom of Beatrex to carry you on your journey

Blue Moon Academy

For more information or to enroll now, go to
www.BlueMoonAcademy.com

CPSIA information can be obtained
at www.ICGtesting.com
Printed in the USA
LVOW05s1051301217
561338LV00004B/8/P